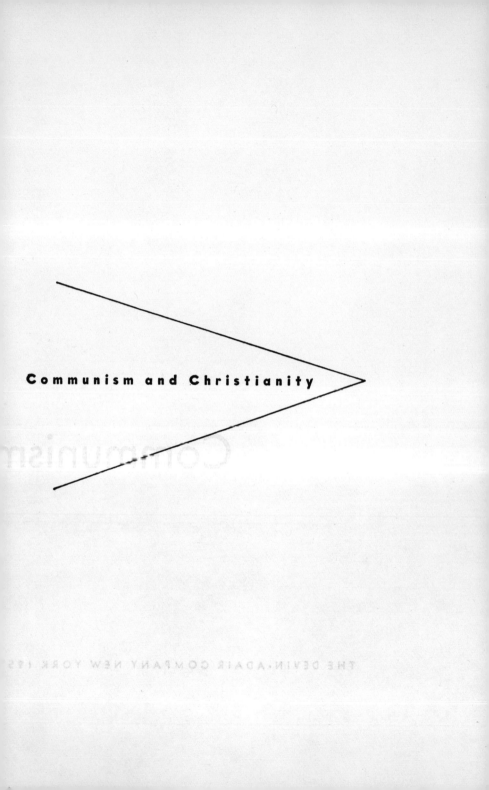

Communism and Christianity

Communism

THE DEVIN-ADAIR COMPANY NEW YORK 195

nd Christianity

MARTIN C. D'ARCY

Canadian Agents: Thomas Nelson & Sons, Ltd., Toronto
Library of Congress catalog card number: 57–13353
Designed by Walter Miles
Manufactured in the United States of America

This book was originally published as a
Penguin Special in 1956 by Penguin Books.

preface to the American edition

Communism has been forced to show its face in the United States of America, and there can be few who are unaware of its hold upon its followers and the methods used for undermining national unity. There are, however, some who distinguish between its baser and accidental elements and the supposed ideals for which it stands, and many know all too little about its philosophy of life. This book is written with the intention of stating as fairly as possible the views which Marx first propagated, views developed and held as sacrosanct by his followers, Lenin and Stalin and the rulers in Russia and China. Once seen for what they are, they can be compared with the Christian view of man and history; and as Christian ideas have entered deeply into European and American social habits, art and law and politics, so we can see what changes with regard to freedom, conscience and human life the Communist creed inevitably entails.

Senator Harry Cain, during a committee hearing,

recently said that far too many among us, having no knowledge of communism whatsoever, are too easily led to believe that certain things are Communist when nothing could be further from the truth. It is a maxim of war, he said, to know one's enemy better than oneself, and this is true of the present struggle with communism. Of course, as many countries have learned by bitter experience, Communist propaganda can appear in sheep's clothing and, in this case also, the lack of knowledge of the true nature of communism can lead all too easily to the belief that things are non-Communist when nothing could be further from the truth.

The United States claims to stand for democracy; the Soviet Union also bespeaks the name. I hope that readers of this book will realize what democracy should mean for those who have any regard for the duties and dignities of the human individual, and how unavailing a materialist philosophy is in the promotion of genuine democracy and that peaceful liberty which is "the tranquility of order" and goodwill. Above all others the citizens of the United States should be well informed of the principles which must govern human institutions, that they may protect what has glorified the past, detect what is in the present situation insidious, and insure the future.

M. C. D'ARCY

September, 1957

contents

introduction

A Christian puts his trust in God, a humanist in the powers of man, a Communist in the productions of nature and the economic use of them. Each of these is said to make his belief into a religion insofar as he is dedicated to it heart and soul, and finds in it the cure of mankind's troubles. Nevertheless, to use the word "religion" to describe humanism sounds far-fetched. Not so with the Communist. Dr. Charles Lowry, for instance, entitles the first chapter of his book, *Communism and Christ*, "Communism—a New Religion." He holds that the use of the word "religion" is correct because Marx went far beyond a mere scientific analysis and theory of economic society; he created a faith and gave the promise of a new destiny for man. "The appeal of Marxism was, and is, twofold. It exploited and exploits the prestige of science, claiming to be a scientific system for a scientific age. It offered, and offers, deliverance from present injustice and misery, promising to all believers a new world of equality and happiness. This gospel of deliverance comes directly to the poor and dispossessed; to the uneasy and idealistic children of privilege it brings vicarious absolution from guilt and participation in righteousness." Hence Marxism is not only a rival to Christianity, but a religious rival; and to show how this is so Dr. Lowry sets side by side their contrasting articles of faith. In this table we have the living God and matter in motion, the Trinity and the dialectic trinity of thesis, antithesis and synthesis, a chosen people and the proletariat, sin and the evil of private property and the exploitation of it, the Church and the Party, the Sacred Scriptures and the Marxist writings, the coming of the kingdom of God and the withering away of the State and the coming of the classless society.

Whether or not Dr. Lowry makes out his assertion, that communism is a religion, he does show that Christianity and communism can be brought sufficiently close together to be compared. Such a comparison I shall try to make, giving, as I hope, a fair statement of the main Communist beliefs and describing so much of Christian doctrine as is relevant to the subject to be discussed. There are difficulties in the way of doing this which I must explain at the very beginning. Like most famous thinkers, Marx has become a bone of contention. After his death there arose different schools of interpretation. That of Lenin has prevailed, but here again we have to make up our minds as to what Lenin held. Stalin always referred to Lenin and treated his writings as sacred, but I need hardly say that Stalin's interpretation is not accepted by all. Stalin used Lenin's authority to denounce deviationists, but no one can be sure that he is not a deviationist, especially if he be an outsider. All that I can pretend is that I have striven to enter into the minds of the makers of communism, to see the logic of their thought, and so to understand why it has made an appeal to so many able and generous minds. In comparing Christianity with it I have had to face two special difficulties. One is that as with communism so with Christianity, there are opposing views of its right meaning. In former days these could be separated into two camps, the Catholic and the Protestant, but since the coming of liberal theology no such simple division will suffice. Many who regard themselves as Christians have abandoned the time-honored explanations of the Creeds, and even assume that Christianity need not be more than an ethical system. One party holds that, if only the Marxists would welcome Christian fellowship, or at least tolerate full religious liberty, Christianity could take on a new life and communism itself become universally acceptable. Others without going so far think that Christianity is too attached to bourgeois social theories and would have it take over the social teaching of Marx on capitalism and property, equality and liberty. There are some, again, who believe that Christians have much to learn from the philosophy of the dialectic and the close connection of theory with practice.

The second difficulty is this. Christianity began as a promise of salvation, the promise, that is, of forgiveness by God of sin, of friendship and union with him in this life and happiness in a new society, the kingdom of God, after death. The message of the Beatitudes is far removed from that of Marx. It is concerned directly with a "kingdom not of this world," and Christ kept deliberately aloof from politics or social crusades or earthly societies. Despite what Dr. Lowry says, if we compare the Christian Creed with the Communist Manifesto there seem to be few points of contact. The first articles of the Creed are about God and his creation, and the Communists do not believe in any God. The next series of articles state that a historical person was both God and man, that he lived and died and rose from the dead. The Communist approach to religion is uniform: all religions are myths invented by a depressed class to compensate for its misery. The historical arguments for the claims of Christ leave the Communist unmoved. The final statements of the Creed refer to an historical organization, the Church, to a society of saints, and to life everlasting. Here alone some writers have noticed a resemblance. They stress the Jewish antecedents of Marx and construe his vision of a classless society as a transvaluation of the Jewish expectation of a Messianic kingdom. The Christian hope of a spiritual kingdom is brought down to earth, and in the light of a scientific economics the victory of the poor, the proletariat of the world, is assured, and the promise given of a perfect earthly society.

Without whittling away the vital differences, however, I hope to show that Christianity and communism do propose comparable answers on many questions. Communism calls religion other-worldly, and it is true that the primary concern of Christianity is "everlasting life." Nevertheless, unlike some mystic religions, it does not turn its back upon human affairs and bid its disciples to escape from them. I will try to show how and why this is so; for the moment it suffices to point to the admitted influence of Christian principles and ideals in the formation of Western society.

The philosophy of life which was responsible for this influence is what I understand by Christianity throughout the book. This, I think, will be expected of a writer who is setting out to compare a relatively new and revolutionary view of man and society with one which, where it is not held explicitly, has nevertheless ordered and controlled our social habits, our laws, the growth of our liberties and the attitude of our fellow men—what, in fact, may be called the Christian conscience. Indeed at a time when so many ideas are in the melting pot and the rallying cry of democracy hides so many controversial beliefs, it is imperative to have a clear idea of what is foremost in the traditions of Western society. In the pages to follow, nevertheless, I have, where necessary, mentioned variant opinions within the Christian outlook, and acknowledge help, even where I am in disagreement, from a book.

M. C. D.

1. COMMUNISM

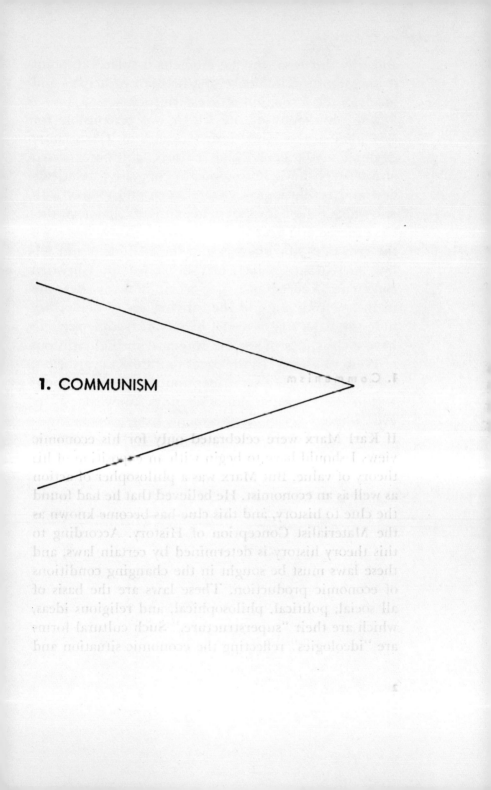

1. Communism

If Karl Marx were celebrated only for his economic views I should have to begin with an exposition of his theory of value. But Marx was a philosopher of action as well as an economist. He believed that he had found the clue to history, and this clue has become known as the Materialist Conception of History. According to this theory history is determined by certain laws, and these laws must be sought in the changing conditions of economic production. These laws are the basis of all social, political, philosophical, and religious ideas, which are their "superstructure." Such cultural forms are "ideologies" reflecting the economic situation and dependent upon it. The truth of this claim will be examined later, but one difficulty must be met immediately. As material economic conditions determine cultural and philosophic ideas, the antecedents to the Marxist theory should be sought in them. But to do this would confuse the issue and be at the same time laborious and unremunerative for the reader. It is simpler and, I think, more intelligible to begin with an account of the ideas of man and nature which preceded those of Marx. Marxist thinkers do at times follow this course, and it does not prejudge the Marxist theory. All the evidence goes to show that Marx applied himself to and benefited by the study of the Hegelian philosophy, and Hegel certainly was much indebted to the thinkers who preceded him. Philosophers influence one another, and there is a history of thought, no matter whether we accept or reject the claim that thought is always due to the economic conditions of the time.

By general consent René Descartes (1596–1650) is held to have had most influence on the course which modern philosophy has followed. This is by reason of the novelty of his method of approach and his sharp division between mind and matter. Mind and matter were by him completely separated, and each was said to have its own distinctive characteristics. Mind or soul was a thinking substance, and it expressed itself in clear and distinct ideas. Matter, on the other hand, he defined as extension. Where matter is, there is extension, and where there is extension, there is matter. The mind is not extended, and matter has nothing in common with mind. These distinctions came at a favorable moment, when human reason was asserting its rights, and advances in the sciences were being made by increased observation and experiment. The assumption that matter was extension fitted in excellently with mathematical techniques, and these techniques proved to be so successful that the original assumptions and distinctions seemed to be fully verified. Newton crowns this scientific approach with his celestial mechanics. The world had been laid bare by his genius, and nature was looked upon as a gigantic piece of mechanics. These successes served, too, to confirm the belief that the mind as reason has no limit. Writers spoke of the age of reason, and belittled the past as a period of infancy when reason was still hampered by fancy and imagination and myth.

By the end of the eighteenth century the advances in science had affected the form of life in, for example, England and France. Feudal life changed into the industrial, and a new class of workers arose living in large cities and producing work in conditions far different from those of the old manual and handicraft workers. So rapid, indeed, was the change that the best minds of the time were disturbed and began to question the assumptions of the Cartesian theory. Nature did not seem to be sufficiently explained in static and mechanical formulae; besides, the new economic forces were out of hand and had upset the old traditional relations between landowners and laborers, merchants and workmen. The sources of wealth were material, so that economists as well as scientists and philosophers were driven to question the assumptions inherited from Descartes. What if mind and matter were not cut off from one another by a hatchet? Mind is motionable, and matter, if extended, is also in motion. Lamarck hit upon the idea of evolution in biology; Adam Smith and Ricardo wrestled with new ideas in economics; the French philosophers, as Plekhanov argued, were on the scent, but failed because of their Cartesian belief in reason. They were alive to the changing conditions of society and realized that human institutions were affected by the social environment. Nevertheless, the old habit of referring everything to reason was still too strong, and many returned to an idealist answer to the social problems which perplexed them. Then came the French Revolution, and the question of the place and growth of man in human institutions became still more pressing. Some went so far as to admit that politics depended on social conditions and on the state of property. They did not, however, in Plekhanov's view, dig deep enough, and ask themselves on what the state of property depended. Instead they contented themselves with vague answers, such as the qualities of human nature. The old confusion about mind and nature and their absolute distinction still lingered on, until their conjunction and identity were pronounced by Fichte, Schilling, Hegel, and then by Marx.

Hegel ends the reign of reason and idealism with a grand display of fireworks. He ends the old idealism, but he also inaugurates the reign of movement, motion, and dialectic, which Darwin was to formulate in terms of evolution, and as the Marxists maintain, Marx perfected in his dialectical materialism. It is difficult for us now to realize the extravagant belief in reason which the engineers of the French Revolution and other movements possessed. Hegel could write of it as follows: "Thought, the concept of law, all at once made itself felt, and against this the old scaffolding of wrong could make no stand. . . . Since the sun had been in the firmament, and the planets circled round it, the sight had never been seen of man standing on his head —i.e., on the idea—and building reality after this image. Anaxagoras first said that Nous, reason, rules the world: but now for the first time, had man come to recognize that the Idea must rule the mental reality. And this was a magnificent sunrise. All thinking beings have participated in celebrating the holy day. A sublime emotion swayed man at that time, an enthusiasm of reason pervaded the world, as if now had come the reconciliation of the Divine principle with the world." In this passage the intoxication of current belief in Reason is marked; marked also is the combination of the Greek idea of reason and the language of Christian theology. It is Nous which rules the world, and Nous reconciles the world of nature with the human reason. Just as sin had separated man from God, so in history nature and man had been divided and the dialectic developed by Hegel served as the mode of reconciliation. Marx belonged to a Jewish family which had become Christian, and the influence of his upbringing can be found in his almost religious conviction that the unrighteous world around him could be righted and a perfect world would in time succeed the evil one which he knew from experience and from all that Engels told him of conditions in industrial England. His studies at Bonn and Berlin were begun with the aim of becoming a lawyer, but his interests were philosophical and social. From the reading of Kant and

Fichte he turned to Hegel, and Hegel made a capital change in his thinking, even as on Kierkegaard, but with such opposite results. Marx was not the man to be interested in ideas for their own sake. The mathematical concepts of his fellow Jew, Spinoza, and the shut-off categories of Kant did not suit his wants. It was Hegel who supplied them partially because he had an interest in history and his system was in movement. The icebound ideas of his predecessors thawed in the Hegelian dialectic and began to flow.

The famous dialectic of Hegel is to be seen most conspicuously at work in history, but there is a faint trace of his early theological education in the language he used, especially in the first formulations of the dialectic. Man is estranged from himself, and therefore sets over against himself what has become estranged or alienated. The individual first thinks of others as hostile or at least as strangers, and it takes time for them to become neighbors and for all to be united in one society. His ideal self also stands over against him and is objectivized as external law to which he is subject. In time, here also the law becomes part of the life of the self, an interior law which means self-perfection. By extending this pregnant idea we come to understand that nature, which Descartes had cut off entirely from the mind, can be reconciled. It is at first the non-self, the object utterly extraneous, but, as we grow in knowledge, this nature becomes more and more intelligible, and shows itself, so far from being hostile to mind, to be embodied reason. Then finally it can be spoken of only as rational and of the same constitution as the mind itself. "The real is the rational and the rational is the real." If then invariably the mind grows to its proper stature by setting over against itself an object and reconciling that object in a richer unity of itself, this must be the very fabric and process of reality, and we have arrived at the secret of true philosophizing. Posit something, say something, let something happen, and in every case the opposite will be generated, and in the overcoming of this opposition an advance will be made. The mind cannot think without an object, and the object in being grasped and mastered by the subject increases the richness of the subject. Here is the law of all mental growth and the key to science, history, philosophy and religion. Throughout the works of Hegel we can watch his principle serving as a formula and a technique of discovery, and as a result he has laid himself open to much criticism and even contempt.

From his principle he tried to deduce what must have happened in history and what will happen, and this attempted short cut to knowledge failed badly, as historians have not been slow to point out. On this point the historians are in agreement with Marx. It is doubtful whether Marx ever completely understood the Hegelian philosophy. When, for instance, he said that "for Hegel the spiritual process which he goes so far as to transform into an independent subject under the name of Idea, is the demiurge of reality, and reality is only its exterior manifestation," he misrepresented Hegel. Reality in Hegel's mind is not the exterior of the Idea but its content. Nevertheless he did fasten on a weakness in the Hegelian system, that is, the tendency to abstract the Idea from the content and the evidence, and so to produce a logic and not a living process. Nor did Marx properly understand what Hegel meant by his dialectic, but he did know how to use what he found useful in what he read of its workings. He was not interested in the pure theory of the dialectic, and as he says in his *Theses on Feuerbach:* "The dispute over the reality or non-reality of thinking which is isolated from practice is a purely scholastic question." What he had learnt from Hegel is set forth by Engels and quoted by Lenin: "The great basic idea that the world is not to be viewed as a complex of fashioned objects, but as a complex of processes, in which apparently stable objects, no less than the images of them inside our heads (our concepts), are undergoing incessant changes, arising here and disappearing there, and which with all apparent accident and in spite of all momentary retrogression, ultimately constitutes a progressive development—this great basic idea, has, particularly since the time of Hegel, so deeply penetrated the general consciousness that hardly anyone will now venture to dispute it in its general form. But it is one thing to accept it in words, quite another thing to put it into practice on every occasion and in every field of operation."

This last sentence sums up the lesson Marx learnt from Hegel and also his disagreement with him. He took over the dialectic because its working seemed to divulge the movement of events and the way they moved, and by keeping his eyes on reality he intended to discard the "idea" and be what he claimed to be, an empiricist and scientist, instead of an idealist. He was helped at this time both by his acquaintance with Engels and his study of Feuerbach.

Marx first met Friedrich Engels in 1842 when Engels was on his way to England. In England the conditions of the workers in Manchester made an ineffaceable impression upon Engels, as can be seen from his words written in 1844, "We have now followed the proletariat of the British Island through all branches of its activity, and found it everywhere living in want and misery under totally inhuman conditions." From 1844 onwards, until Marx died, he became the ideal friend and supporter of Marx, combining with him in the Manifesto and other writings, and at times expressing the ideas of Marx better than Marx did himself. Moreover his experience of industrial conditions was of great value in supplying Marx with evidence. Feuerbach had begun as an Hegelian, but grew skeptical of the lofty idealism in it. Hegel had made God into an immanent spirit who brings back what is opposed to spirit in the developing thought of man. That is the reason why so many have rejected the religious ideas of Hegel as pantheist. Hegel had his answers. These answers, however, to Feuerbach's mind, take away what is human and individual in life and dissipate it in the unreal and abstract Idea. Thought is not something by itself, not even when it begins with a capital letter. It is an activity of human beings which depends upon the experience we have of reality. To Hegel thought is creative; to Feuerbach thought is conditioned by the real. The real comes before thought. We human beings are, moreover, body as well as mind, and as creatures of nature we are the product of nature, of culture, and of history, and far more affected by the body than the idealists allow. Feuerbach, therefore, forsakes the Idea and with it religion. Religion is replaced by the love between man and man and their mutual relations in society. He is a humanist with a bias, where needed, to materialism, and he explains religion as a myth constructed by man to compensate for the disappointments and hardships of life.

Feuerbach's teaching helped Marx to bring into focus the thoughts which were thronging in his mind. Feuerbach had, as he thought, shown up the false element in Hegel's system, the intrusion, that is, of the Absolute Idea careering through history without regard for what was real. He had also suggested an explanation of the hold of religion on men's minds. But he had stopped short. He had not shown why men should have to compensate for their miseries by inventing a paradisal land; and no explanation would suffice without taking into account the precise nature of that misery. It came from the misuse of property and from the exploitation of the landless and the worker. Again Feuerbach substituted human society for God and religious worship, but once more he cramped himself by looking to politics and political equality as the cure for human troubles. Marx felt that Feuerbach, like so many of the older political thinkers and economists, was still tainted with idealism and liberalism. They could not answer the fundamental questions, whose answer lay embedded in the conditions of the exploited poor of Manchester. Hegel had gone dreadfully wrong by confusing political sovereignty with the people and divinizing the existing Prussian state, and Feuerbach tended to make the same mistake. What was wanted was a true brotherhood of man, and it must be no mere phrase, but truth and human nobility shining from their labor-hardened forms. He now saw before him an answer which took in everything, a scientific theory which was operative and not just a theory, a form of action which descended into matter and out of this living matter directed the determinate forces which ruled nature and the animal kingdom and man, a dialectic materialism which could supersede the old vague and utopian philosophies.

This new philosophy was, however, to be unlike the old. He had written of Feuerbach and said firmly that he was not interested in purely theoretical questions because they were a waste of time. "The question whether objective truth is an attribute of human thought is not a theoretical but a practical question." Philosophy must be active and even revolutionary, and he was sure that he had found the clue in what he called dialectical materialism. Marx has at times been treated as if his contribution to thought lay in his economic or social views. But as Professor Hodges has written: "It is that, but it is also much more. Lenin, in his account of the origin of Marxism, presents Marx as the heir not only of British political economy and French socialism but also of German philosophy, and he puts the philosophy first of the three. He is right." It is for this reason we can dispense with a full account of his economic theory. The dialectic can be outlined without any such account; and moreover it is the philosophy and not the economic theory which stands as a rival interpretation of life to that of Christianity. In as much, however, as the economic theory fits into the general philosophy, and helps to justify his claim that his philosophy is empirical and down to earth, a brief explanation of it must be given.

Marx, out of his reading of Ricardo and Adam Smith, developed a theory of value of his own. Adam Smith transmitted his optimism to Marx, but not the grounds for it. Smith spoke for the liberal creed that unrestricted self-interest in the economic sphere was bound in the long run to be to the advantage of all. Free competition served the common good. This Marx flatly denied, proclaiming that the exact opposite was bound to happen, the destruction of the bourgeois society and the advent of the proletariat. But while he criticized Adam Smith on this count he learnt from his theory of value the distinction, also made by Ricardo, between two kinds of economic value, use value and exchange value. He seems to vary at times in his definition of exchange value. Whatever else he intended by the expression he certainly meant at least a property of a thing in virtue of which it could be exchanged, and the value of this commodity must be gauged by the amount of labor needed to produce it. He is at pains to try to show that whether a laborer is lazy or diligent this definition of value can be proved to hold true, and again he maintains that the difference between skilled and unskilled labor does not upset his definition. It follows from what he has said that the workers create the whole value of the goods and services which are sold, and, as is obvious, they do not retain the value of their work. Part of the value is paid to them in wages and salaries, and this is, in the capitalist system, the amount which is needed to keep them fit for their work. If then all that is needed to keep them fit can be done in five hours' labor, and the laborer works for ten hours, the laborer is getting only half of the value which he himself produces. This half left over Marx calls surplus value, and his complaint is that this is appropriated by the capitalist. In other words the capitalist system is built on exploitation of the worker and injustice. This theory of values is still part of the Communist Bible, but the doctrine is not dependent on it, no more than the power to walk depends on a particular pair of shoes. It fits the movement of the dialectic, and it is more to the point here to show how it works into the general pattern. The first important attempt by Marx to display that pattern is in his essay *National Economy,* written in 1844. Of this an excellent summary is given by Mr. A. C. MacIntyre in his *Marxism: an Interpretation.* He begins by arguing that former writers have been mistaken by taking private property as their starting point. Economics does not depend upon the relations arising from such property. "The worker cannot produce without nature, without the world of sense. It is the material through which his labor realizes itself, in which it is active, from which and by means of which it is productive." Marx is here moving away from the common assumptions and playing up his theory of labor. He insists that besides the labor which produces commodities, there is the laborer himself who becomes a commodity. To explain this he resorts to the early Hegelian doctrine of estrangement and reconciliation, a doctrine which has religious associations. When man becomes a worker he becomes

14

estranged from himself and regards himself as an object and commodity. Work, he writes, "the activity of life, the productive life, appears to man as a means to supply a need, the need of maintaining physical existence." This very estrangement, however, does serve the purpose of making him conscious of being a man. He stands over against himself, becoming aware of his estrangement, separated both from his labor and his fellow men. During this period of estrangement he gives a false personality to that which is really his own estranged self. He creates religion, the world of gods more powerful than himself ("The more man places in God, the less he retains in himself"). He creates, too, the world of property and ownership. "National economy begins with labor as the true soul of production and nevertheless gives labor nothing and private property everything." This alienation is heightened and reaches to its fall and end in the growth of industrialism. The worker ceases to own anything except his labor, becomes himself a commodity, the while the capitalist makes more and more profits and accumulates property; until at length he who creates all the power by his labor is at the mercy of the bourgeois owner. This is the present position, and it is one which has been analyzed wrongly by the economists. Adam Smith holds on to private property, Proudhon wishes to abolish private property without understanding the implications of property and social relations. The crude Communist does not think beyond his nose, never seeing that the mere destruction of private property does not of itself provide a truly human life. Alone Marx has hit, so he thinks, on the real flaw of present-day society and can produce the cure. That consists in ending the estrangement of man from himself. Only in the socialist society which understands the meaning of labor, the reliance on nature and production and the reconciliation of man with himself and his neighbor, only in such a society "does his natural existence coincide with his human existence, and nature exist for men."

The views of this youthful Marx, both in outlook and tone, are far from those which are accepted as Marxian. They are more humanistic than scientific and have religious overtones. The outlook expressed is later covered over by materialistic and scientific language, but it remains in his thought and is therefore of great importance for a judgment on Marx. It is as if the Jew in him were in protest against the dilettantism of the liberal thinkers. He comes announcing a kingdom of man and preaches a revolution which will bring about the perfect society. This revolutionary zeal is hidden later by his proud belief that he was, unlike his fellow socialists, first and foremost a scientist drawing his conclusions from empirical evidence. The religious language of estrangement and reconciliation changes in the next few years into what he thinks an exact interpretation of the changes produced by changing conditions of production. In *The German Ideology* he dismisses the idealists as follows: "They have conceived the whole process which we have outlined as the revolutionary process of 'man,' so that at every historical stage 'man' was substituted for the individuals and shown as the motive force of history. The whole process was thus conceived as a process of the self-estrangement of 'man.' " He prefers now to talk in the language of labor and its relations to capital, and he repudiates any form of mysticism or even moral purpose. As MacIntyre says justly: "Marx wishes now to speak of *what is* rather than *what ought to be*"; and he goes on to quote from Engels' preface to the English edition in 1881 of the Communist Manifesto to illustrate his remark. "The Manifesto being our joint production, I consider myself bound to state that the fundamental proposition which forms its nucleus, belongs to Marx. That proposition is: That in every historical epoch, the prevailing mode of economic production and exchange and the social organization following from it, form the basis upon which is built up, and from which alone can be explained, the political and intellectual history of that epoch; that consequently the whole history of mankind (since the dissolution of primitive tribal society, holding land in common ownership) has been a history of class struggles, contests between exploiting and exploited, ruling and oppressed classes; that the history of these class struggles forms a series of evolutions in which, now adays, a stage has been reached where the exploited and oppressed class—the proletariat—cannot attain its emancipation from the sway of the exploiting and ruling class—the bourgeoisie—without at the same time, and once and for all, emancipating society at large from all exploitation, oppression, class distinction, and class struggles."

This is full blown Marxism, and it is this kind of Marxism, more than the preliminary sketches, which has to be examined in any comparison of Marxism and

Christianity. It will be observed how the earlier language about man's estrangement and reconciliation with himself and with his fellow men has disappeared. The perfect society is promised, but it is not promised to humanity but to a class, namely, that of the workers or proletariat. The Manifesto has a political sound, as political as the *Marseillaise* at the time of the French Revolution. Some critics have been shocked at this, and think that the change from man or humanity to the class of workers makes of Marxism nothing more than a political creed. That Marx is addressing himself to the workers is obvious, but he would justify himself by science and by facts. By a class Marx did not mean a political party always conscious of its plight and its unity. It may be quite unconscious of its common interests, but it exists and necessarily exists because of the dialectical laws of history. The conditions of production are such that they create classes, and in the conditions which Marx was envisaging, in fact, the vast majority of the inhabitants of the world belong to the proletariat and the time has come when they must unite and bring the bourgeois dominance to an end. He tells us what he means by the proletariat in the Manifesto. "The proletariat movement is the self-conscious, independent movement of the immense majority, in the interest of the immense majority. The proletariat, the lowest stratum of our present society, cannot stir, cannot raise itself up, without the whole superincumbent strata of official society being sprung into the air." The movement this time is a self-conscious one, because now at last the people, instead of being carried along without knowing how or why by the forces of nature and economics, are able to exercise their freedom by understanding the necessity of events, and, therefore, they will be able to avoid the old conflicts and by controlling the laws of life reach a peaceful term to the long warfare which has preceded the new classless society.

2. THE ESSENCE OF MARXISM

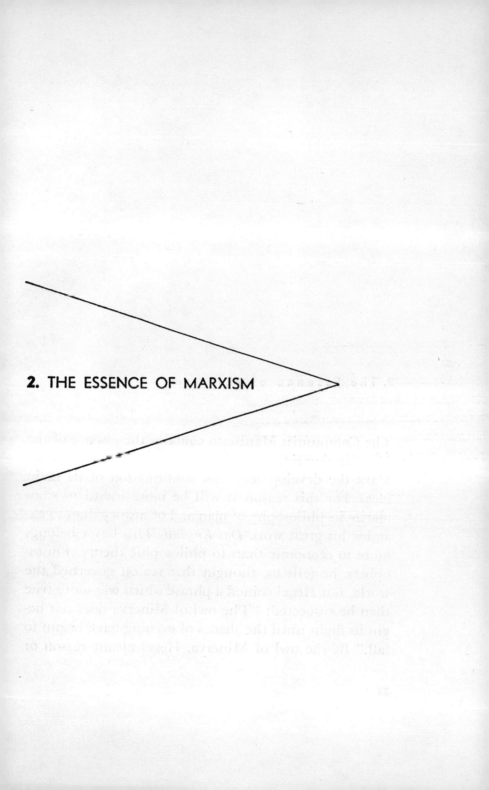

2. The Essence of Marxism

The Communist Manifesto contains the essence of the Marxian doctrine, and the succeeding years meant for Marx the development and confirmation of its main ideas. For this reason it will be more useful to summarize its philosophy of man and of history than to examine his great work *Das Kapital*. This latter belongs more to economic than to philosophic theory. Philosophers, he tells us, thought that reason governed the world, but Hegel coined a phrase which was more true than he suspected: "The owl of Minerva does not begin its flight until the shades of evening have begun to fall." By the owl of Minerva, Hegel meant reason or wisdom; but the recognition of conformity to law in the flights of the owl of Minerva was the foundation of quite a new view of history and of the intellectual development of mankind. It is not reason which gives birth and growth to the laws of nature; it is the laws of nature which determine the thinking of the mind. Work is done in the sunshine; the owl of reason starts its flight late in the shadows of evening. In other words, we must look to material reality for the source and nature of our ideas. Our ideas depend upon the material situation, and, as will be shown, the conditions of life or production at any given epoch. Other ideas, religious, moral, and political, are a superstructure built on the life we are living and living necessarily. Nature is determined and is also in movement; it has its laws, and as man is a creature of nature he cannot escape its laws. Nor would it be sensible for him to try to do so. He has one advantage over inanimate matter; he is conscious and he is a tool-bearing animal. He can, therefore, bring about changes in nature, and these changes involve him in a new series of causes and effects which he had not intended or even surmised. "When an elephant breaks off a branch to brush away flies, the change effected may be considered unimportant. Not so, however, when man becomes a tiller of the soil." At this stage men produce something and in "the social production which men carry on, they enter into definite relations that are indispensable and independent of their will; these relations of production correspond to a definite stage of development of their material forces of production. The sum total of these relations of production constitutes the economic structure of society, the real foundation on which rises a legal and political superstructure." What man thinks is, therefore, determined by the material conditions, but this, so far from being what anti-Marxists think, a condemnation of the whole theory, makes for solid good sense and progress. Marx had been very struck by a saying of Hegel: "World history is progress in the essence of freedom, progress which we must understand in its necessity." He interpreted this to mean that "freedom is the recognition of necessity. Necessity is blind only in so far as it is not understood." By such an interpretation he was able to fasten the history of man to a materialist foundation, and at the same time justify his own active program. The economic forces which man sets going are equally determined with those of nature, but it is within the capacity of man to understand them and thereby attain true freedom. This view is clearly set out by Engels.

"Active social forces work exactly like natural forces; blindly, forcibly, destructively so long as we do not understand and reckon with them. But when once we understand them, when once we grasp their action, their direction, their effects, it depends only upon ourselves to subject them more and more to our own will, and by means of them to reach our own ends. And this holds quite especially of the mighty productive forces of to-day. As long as we obstinately refuse to understand the nature and the character of these social means of action—and this understanding goes against the grain of the capitalist mode of production and its defenders— so long these forces are at work in spite of us, in opposition to us, so long they master us, as we have shown in detail.

"But when once their nature is understood, they can, in the hands of the producers working together, be transformed from master demons into willing servants. The difference is as that between the destructive force of electricity in the lightning of the storm, and electricity under command in the telegraph and the voltaic arc; the difference between a conflagration, and fire working in the service of man. With this recognition at last of the real nature of the productive forces of to-day, the social anarchy of production gives place to a social regulation of production upon a definite plan according to the needs of the community and of each individual."

It will be observed that Marx and Engels here suppose that the laws which govern nature and human society are understood, for it is only on this supposition that they can be sure that their analysis of the history of man and their predictions of what is to come can be true. Their explanation of human freedom also rests on the same supposition. They shared the confidence of the scientists of the nineteenth century, and Marx felt that instead of the windy discourses of the idealist philosophers he himself was keeping to observed facts and to strict scientific generalizations. Material reality and sense experience are the only safe courts of appeal in any inquiry. Physical nature had revealed its laws and shown itself to be in flux according to a definite rhythm, a rhythm which he identified with that perfected by Hegel and called the dialectic. That matter, and indeed all reality, is the result of friction, the meeting of opposites, had been held by the Greek philosopher, Heraclitus. Aristotle also, whom Marx admired, had explained material substance and substantial change in terms of matter and form, and living changes in terms of passing away and coming to be. Dialectic, however, as the word suggests, was invented to describe a method of advance in argument. Let a view be challenged by a denial or an assertion of its opposite, and out of the discussion a better definition or idea could emerge which preserved what had been true in the imperfect statements made at first by both disputants. This method was brought to a high finish by Socrates. Hegel was not the first of modern philosophers to resurrect the dialectic, but no one used it to such effect as he or made it such a cardinal feature of his system. Hegel's use was not a complete break with that of the Platonic writers because he applied it principally to the movement of thought.

Dialectic expresses the way the mind works; it is the very procedure whereby it arrives at truth. In an imperfect stage the mind finds itself confronted with various apparently conflicting truths or aspects of truth; this conflict has to be resolved, and at each resolution the mind is richer and nearer to a grasp of truth itself. At the end all the errors have been shed, the half truths have been corrected, and the harmony of full truth is seen in all its beauty. That dialectic in this sense should be thought of as the happiest and perhaps the only way of making the warp and woof of knowledge is reasonable. Marx, however, transferred this mental operation to the processes of nature, and claimed that nature too, and for him this meant all reality, consisted of a dialectical movement. If the use of the word appears strange there does appear nevertheless something in the processes of nature corresponding to the thrust and riposte of intellectual discussion. Matter is in movement, and scientists use the language and the hypothesis of opposites, of positive and negative. From these opposites come new combinations and these can be compared with the thesis, the antithesis, and the resulting synthesis of thought. Professor Hodges makes sense of this dialectical process of inanimate nature when he writes: "But what if the laws of nature are not mechanical, but dialectical? This will mean that nothing is simple, for everything is a product of the interaction of opposite forces, and so contains a tension or conflict within itself; and nothing is self-contained, for everything is what it is in great measure because of its surroundings, and when anything enters into changed relationships it is itself changed. Everywhere is energy, movement, and opposition, and the oppositions are creative. Out of the meeting and struggle of opposite forces and tendencies comes at last a synthesis which contains something of both but is richer than either. This is what dialectic means."

As Marx has committed himself wholeheartedly to a materialistic view of the universe of reality, he is bound to attach great importance to the presence of the dialectic in nature. He saw his philosophy as coherent in all its parts, and the foundation as material reality and dialectical materialism. Once he had established that incontrovertibly he could go on to apply consistently and scientifically the dialectic to economics and to history. Many reading of his explanation of history might suppose that here was a hypothesis like any other hypothesis invented to organize the facts of history, but they would be mistaken. No doubt Marx's passion for the social improvement of man and his crusading ardor for the salvation of the worker lie at the back of his philosophy, with the result that communism is often regarded as a social theory and little more. But Marx meant his view to be the complete answer to life and to its problems, to be a philosophy which was complete in its truth and the fulcrum to change the world. His dialectic of history is meant to be both philosophically and scientifically certain; and all that happens proceeds inevitably from the ground truth that matter is in motion and obeys a dialectical principle. This foundation firmly laid, then he could go on to show that man too obeyed the same principles, that the idealists were quite wrong in appealing to reason or the Absolute Idea or God as a first principle or explanation. Man is just as materialistic as physical or living matter, and once we have looked for what differentiates man from other materialistic forms we can then go on to apply the dialectical method and determine the laws which operate in his development. Now what differentiates man from other animals is that he is tool-bearing. With a certainty, therefore, far beyond that of any hypothesis we must look to what man does with his tools in order to discover how his history will be determined. This means that instead of the usual theories to be found in the books by the liberal or philosophical historians we can work out a scientific explanation in terms of production and the productive forces initiated by many men producing together.

According to Marx the natural history of man is as follows. In the process of evolution, apes which had subsisted on the products of nature around them reached a level at which they began to work upon nature instead of just living on it. In this new form of activity they developed tools, and, as animals live in herds, they formed first an ethnic group, then a matriarchal and finally a patriarchal kind of primitive society. In time in the development of various techniques the simple society was broken up, and those who possessed the greater skills exploited their ability and began to dominate the others. The hunter, the fisherman, the shepherd with the greater skill and power begins to find that his own interests clash with those of the community, and again those who after owning tools come to own land, hire the less skillful to work upon the land and thereby increase their own power. The clash between classes is now unescapable, for, as Marx maintains, the forces let loose by the action of men in their interaction with nature pass beyond the intention and control of those who initiated them and determine the nature of the society and the ideas which prevail. "The social power, that is, the multiplied productive force, which arises through the co-operation of different individuals as it is determined within the division of labor, appears to these individuals, since their co-operation is not voluntary but natural, not as their own united power but as an alien force existing outside them, of the origin and end of which they are ignorant, which they thus cannot control, which on the contrary passes through a peculiar series of phases and stays independent of the will and action of man, nay even being the prime governor of them." Plekhanov sums up the forces by saying that once social relations arise further development takes place by its own inner laws. Dependence on environment becomes indirect instead of direct. There will, of course, be much variation in different places, but always the social environment determines the form of society, and this leads to more and more complex social relationships, and the producer becomes the slave of his own creation. This subjection is, however, finally overcome when man reaches that stage of self-consciousness which enables him to understand the laws which determine historical progress. Here with the knowledge of necessity comes freedom.

Marx distinguishes five periods of society. I have already touched on the earliest, that of primitive communism, and the second, that of patriarchy. The next is feudalism, which is characterized by the separation and antagonism of two classes, the landowner with his private property and the peasant who is the direct producer but tied to the land. He does not benefit from his own work and production. This conflict passed in the sixteenth century into the class struggle of capitalism and labor. The means of production came to be concentrated into the hands of a few who exploited the masses. It is to this latter struggle that Marx pays most attention. He refers to it in the well-known passage from the Communist Manifesto. "The history of all hitherto existing society is the history of class struggles. Freeman and slave, patrician and plebeian, lord and serf, guild master and journeyman, in a word, oppressor and oppressed, stood in constant opposition to one another, carrying on an uninterrupted, now hidden, now open fight, a fight that each time ended, either in a revolutionary reconstitution of society at large, or in the ruin of the contending classes. . . . The modern bourgeois society that has sprouted from the ruins of feudal society has not done away with class antagonisms. It has but established new classes, new conditions of oppression, new forms of struggle in place of the old ones. Our epoch, the epoch of the bourgeoisie, possesses, however, this distinctive feature; it has simplified the class antagonisms. Society as a whole is more and more splitting up into two hostile camps, into two great classes directly facing each other—bourgeoisie and proletariat."

The outstanding contribution of Marx in the economic field is his study of this latter-day struggle. This is not the place to dwell on its purely economic and social features, but as an illustration of dialectical materialism a few points must be mentioned. The changing conditions of production ended the feudal period and introduced capitalism and the rule of the bourgeoisie. The discovery of new sources of raw material, the growth of new techniques, which science steadily improved, for converting them into articles of use, the consequent growth of factories and urbanization, the emergence of a monetary system, created the class of merchantmen and of big business and the congregating of vast hordes of workers in the cities with no interest of their own in the work which they produced. This system of capitalism made immense strides at the end of the eighteenth century and in the nineteenth in the life-time of Marx. The market for goods was expanding and as a result the manufacturers came more and more into competition with one another in the effort to sell their goods. This competition increased the need of the capitalists to cut costs and increase the productivity of their goods. This they could do by improving machinery and lessening the number of employees, and by lowering wages and selling at high prices. Such a step was fatal in the long run to their own interests because the workers became more and more unable to buy back the goods they had produced. What the workers sought was in direct opposition to the aims of the employers. They demanded high wages and low prices. They were also constantly threatened with the misery of unemployment, since it was to the interest of the capitalist to have the whiphand over labor, to have a surplus pool of labor and buy labor at his own price. Reducing wages and selling at a profit had its own fatal effect on the market and led to the repeated phases of depression during the nineteenth century and the consequent increase of unemployment. Perforce the working class united together to protect their interests and formed labor unions which entered into a class struggle with the employers.

This story of capitalism has been summed up by Engels as follows. The "severance of the producer from the means of production. Condemnation of the worker to wage labor for life. *Antagonism between the proletariat and the bourgeoisie.* Growing predominance and increasing effectiveness of the laws governing the production of commodities. Unbridled competition. *Contradiction between socialized organization in the individual factory and social anarchy in production as a whole."* He then speaks of "unheard of development of productive forces, excess of supply over demand, over-production, glutting of the markets, crises every ten years, the vicious circle—excess here, of means of production and products—excess there, of laborers, without employment and without means of existence. But these two levers of production and of social well-being are unable to work together because the capitalist form of production prevents the productive forces from circulating, unless they are first turned into capital—which their very superabundance prevents. The contradiction has grown into an absurdity. *The mode of production rises in rebellion against the form of exchange. . . . "* The partial recognition of this state of affairs by the capitalists leads to the "taking over of the great institutions for production and communication, first by joint stock companies, later on by trusts, then by the state. The bourgeoisie is thus demonstrated to be a superfluous class. All its social functions are now performed by salaried employees." Engels then comes to the Marxist conclusion, the solution and finale of the dramatic history of the class struggles. "The proletariat seizes the public power, and by means of this transforms the socialized means of production, slipping from the hands of the bourgeoisie, into public property. By this act, the proletariat frees the means of production from the character of capital they have thus far borne, and gives their socialized character complete freedom to work itself out. Socialized production upon a predetermined plan becomes henceforth possible. The development of production makes the existence of different classes of society thenceforth an anachronism. In proportion as anarchy in social production vanishes, the political authority of the state dies out. Man, at last the master of his own form of social organization, becomes at the same time the lord over nature, his own master—free."

In this passage from Engels, as also in the preceding summary of history according to Marx, the determining effect of the changing conditions of production, the struggle between classes and the dialectic process are conspicuous. Engels gives the finishing touch to the class struggle in his prophecy of the dictatorship of the proletariat, the withering away of the state and full communism in the classless society. It should be noted that Marx and Engels present their interpretation of history as a scientific one. The passion which heats the language might lead the reader to think that he is listening to a partisan stirring up hatred from a political platform. Certainly the scientific analysis was not intended as mere theory. Marxism is always theory lived and to be put into practice. Nevertheless he proffers the class struggle as a fact of history, and as a scientific historian he should claim that he is not passing moral judgments or expressing his own beliefs and desires. When he writes of the workers and of the class struggle he does not mean that the workers at any particular time are themselves conscious of their interests and the need for organization into one group. In fact the workers have been in many periods both disunited and belonging to different camps, and it is a notorious fact that the poor have often had ambitions to belong to the class of the landowner or the capitalist. What Marx is insisting on is that in, for example, a bourgeois society the material conditions of production are such that one group, the employees, are bound by necessity to be in opposition to the manufacturers, who, to keep the system going, are forced economically to deprive them of the value of their labor. The dialectic movement, too, is a fact and is not supposed to be imposed upon the changes in history. Each change comes about by the opposition of one class with another, and that opposition arises out of the material situation and the conditions and forces of production. The opposition reaches its height and the old order collapses giving place to a new, which in turn, owing to the forces of production, starts anew the struggle between two classes. As Engels asserted, the class struggle in the last phase, that of capitalism, has a characteristic absent from all the former struggles. The workers comprise far the larger part of mankind, and they have become in this last struggle more conscious of their needs and their power. The breakdown of the capitalistic system has meant the taking over by the state of more and more of the means of production. This taking over, however, is still bourgeois in act and in intention. The state is by no means the same as society, and there must come a revolutionary movement in which the workers themselves take over and enter into their inheritance. During this phase a dictatorship is necessary. The old capitalist groups have acquired such strength that they cannot be ousted without force. In the face of such an enemy a dictatorship is required which also disciplines the working class to its responsibilities and co-ordinates its strength.

Marx, living before the successful revolution in Russia, lays down a doctrine of change from capitalism to communism. But, as might be expected, he could not foresee that Russia would be the first country to embrace his ideal, nor was he clear as to the extent that force would be needed. At one time he thought that the ground was so prepared in England that the transition to communism might be peaceful. Where revolution was required and a dictatorship had to be set up he was vague as to the length of time this dictatorship must last. On all these matters Lenin was much more decisive. It is to Lenin we must turn, as will be explained later, if we wish to understand the function of revolution, of the formation of a party and of the dictatorship of the proletariat. Lenin realized, when he had taken command of a socially backward people, that "the liberation of the oppressed class is impossible, not only without a violent revolution, but also without the destruction of the apparatus of state power which was created by the ruling class." Marx was convinced that the proletarian revolution would be different from all other changes, because the people of the world would now be their own masters, "self-conscious" and free, as Engels said. In such a situation the state which had been an organ of the minority for the oppression of the many would no longer be needed, and life would be lived in the service of the community. He saw too that before the estrangement of the people from themselves could be ended there must be a revolutionary class or party which would reduce all opposition and provide the techniques for communism proper. But when the revolution had taken place the foes around the new Russia possessed vast strength, and the conditions within the country were chaotic and in many places recalcitrant. Hence the dictators of the proletariat have to use the instruments at hand of power "both for the purpose of crushing the resistance of the exploiters and for the purpose of guiding the great mass of the population—the peasantry, the petty-bourgeoisie, the semi-proletariat, in the work of organizing Socialist economy." In this stage the worker will receive according to the work he has performed, and not until the final stage is reached will each give according to his ability and receive according to his needs. Lenin had to change his mind on the length of time this transitional period would last. He had in early days spoken of a "lengthy period;" in 1918 he thought "ten years or more" would suffice, but before he died he became more pessimistic.

What Lenin never doubted—no more than Marx—was that the perfect classless society would come. This happy ending to the story of man is a sacred tenet of Marxism. Critics of communism have girded at it for contradicting its own belief; they accuse it of resting on a party, of being a form of tyranny and of not practicing what it preaches. Such criticism has its answer provided by Marxist principles. The time may be longer than expected before pure communism can be practiced, but the fault does not lie with the Marxist leaders. They regard themselves as unable to carry out what they intend by the implacable opposition of the capitalist powers, which are always trying to undo them. For this reason they have to exercise a ruthless warfare against the enemies of communism. Beset by foes they have to make of the U.S.S.R. a war camp in which all other considerations must be put second to the fight for survival and for victory over the imperialist powers. This is the justification for the strict dictatorship and the persecution of deviationists.

The happy ending after the long and necessary struggle of classes within the State is the classless society. This is the scientific prediction of Marxism. For the first time in history the people will have the power and be sufficiently self-conscious to use it properly. The state, which has always so far been an instrument of a minority and an oppressor, will wither away because there will no longer be any need of it. "The mass of the people rises to independent participation . . . in the everyday administration of affairs." Man, who has for so long been estranged from himself and has set up against himself an external deity and law and state, will recognize himself in these externalized objects; necessity and freedom will come together, for this knowledge of necessity will make man one with nature and truly self-determining. It is an ideal which has attracted many. Dr. Lowry quotes the enthusiastic words of a privately-printed work by a Communist writer, William Z. Foster: "The proletarian revolution is the most profound of all revolutions in history. It initiates changes more rapid and far-reaching than in the whole experience of mankind. The hundreds of millions of workers and peasants, striking off their age-old chains of slavery, will construct a society of liberty and prosperity and intelligence. Communism will inaugurate a new era for the human race . . . [it] will bring about the immediate or eventual solution of many great social problems . . . war, religious superstition, prostitution, famine, pestilence, crime, poverty, alcoholism, unemployment, illiteracy, race and national chauvinism, the suppression of women, and every form of slavery and exploitation of one class by another. . . ."

This ecstatic paean is far removed from the realism of a Lenin or Stalin, but it shows how entrancing to some is the Marxist vision. Marx himself dropped the semi-religious language and the prophetic tone from his description of what was to come. He preferred to think of his prediction as a scientific one which dealt with facts and not moral ideals, with what will be and not with what ought to be. The moral fervor, however, can always be felt, and it is this which has caused writers to call his vision a Jewish and messianic one, and to accuse him of falling into contradiction. Certainly at first glance there does seem to be a contradiction between the universal law of dialectical movement and growth and the peaceful condition which the Communist society will enjoy. If growth is necessarily by opposites even in the order of physical reality, how can opposites be absent in the reality of the future? The criticism, as I have said, does not take the Marxist unaware. His answer is that in the growth of society the forces of production set men against themselves and against each other, and they were of such a kind that they swept man along without his being aware of where he was being carried. In this division, which involved conflict, the few were the exploiters of the many. But the struggle reached its penultimate stage in the capitalist crisis, because the proletariat, which comprises the vast majority of mankind, was forced into union, and, in the collapse of the capitalist system, the workers of the world, who can conveniently be regarded as the whole of society, will for the first time in history be masters of their fate. It is this conjunction which sets a term to the dialectic of opposites, and it is for this reason that Marx so treasured the gnomic saying of Hegel that freedom lay in the knowledge of necessity. When the workers of the world are united and have the power to manage their own affairs, and when they have the knowledge how to use the laws of economics and of history, they are free for the first time, and in that freedom they reach the one happiness open to man.

3. LENIN AND STALIN

3. Lenin and Stalin

A system of thought and action so ambitious and so vast in its stretch as Marx's was almost bound to lend itself to different interpretations. The great philosophies of the past, such as those of Plato and Aristotle and Kant, have had disciples of different schools. Marx has been no exception, and his attempt to unite theory and practice, to despise pure theory and at the same time create a kind of bible which should be sacrosanct, led immediately after his death to disputes about his meaning. Engels still survived, and as he had worked so selflessly and with such harmony with Marx and cooperated in his work, his comments and verdicts should naturally have been accepted as the most orthodox. Engels's rendering has always been accepted as most valuable; but as he grew older he seems to have come more and more to regard the work of Marx as a system, scientific and philosophic, and only secondarily as a method of revolution, or thought in action, an electric current always turned on. The scientific side of Marxism appealed to Kautsky, Hilferding and others, so that what they say looks more like an explanation of how history has been made than a means for making history. This "astronomical Marxism," as it was called by the more revolutionary groups, is well illustrated in Hilferding's statement that "Marxism is only a theory of the laws of movement of society formulated in general terms by the Marxian conception of history; the Marxian economics applying in particular to the period of commodity production." Bernstein, on the other hand, being a neo-Kantian, brought out the suppressed moral teaching and reacted against the Relativism of morals which was commonly accepted as part of Marx's teaching. He was all in favor, too, of a peaceable progress or evolution in place of the violence of revolutionary methods. This was in direct opposition to the view of Sorel, who has often been accused of "decomposing Marx." Sorel adopted the activist element, the Marxian cry: "Philosophers have hitherto only interpreted the world; now it for us to *change* the world." He, therefore, set out to change the world by action, that is, by revolutionary action, and to dispense with parliamentarism and social democracy.

These disputes within the party and outside it remained verbal until the Russian Revolution gave the prestige of success and also the power to Lenin and his followers. That the other views did not die easily is, however, shown by the quarrels which continued among the leaders of the new Russian republics, the heresy hunting and the trials. Lenin was determined to hold together the various strands in the doctrine of Marx. He was twitted by perhaps the ablest of Marxist writers, Plekhanov, of turning Marxism into a program of action and neglecting the theoretical side. In fact, however, Lenin was more interested in philosophy than Marx and brought the philosophic ideas of Marx into line with more modern scientific ideas. He also insisted on the ideas of Marx being regarded as more than a science and more than a pragmatic sanction for action. The Marxist writings were to be regarded as the canonical scriptures and no revision or correction was to be permitted. "This philosophy of Marxism is like a steel tapping: it is impossible to remove any fundamental premise, any single part, without involving the loss of objective truth." Marxism is to supersede all the religious and philosophical theories of life which had served man up to the time of his coming. "The Marxian doctrine is omnipotent because it is true. It is complete and harmonious, and provides men with an integral world conception which is irreconcilable with any form of superstition, reaction, or defense of bourgeois oppression. It is the legitimate successor of the best that was created by humanity in the nineteenth century, in the shape of German philosophy, English political economy, and French socialism."

The problem for Lenin was, while keeping rigidly to the text of Marx, to match with it the courses of action almost forced on him by the novel situation in which he found himself in a country predominantly peasant and surrounded by strong enemies. The material conditions of the workers, also, had changed in many countries as well as the economic and scientific ideas. What he is credited with is the development of the Marxist philosophy, the putting of it to the test in concrete action. It was clear that the change over from capitalism could not be accomplished by the rapid collapse of the latter and the peaceful occupation of the decadent bourgeois states. This historic fact had to be accounted for, and Lenin does it in his *Imperialism*. He calls imperialism the transitional stage to socialism, one in which "moribund capitalism" turns more and more monopolistic. The industries pass into the hands of a group of oligarchs who take over the control of the banks. This group of financiers have their finger in every pie all over the world, and they export capital and by the power of money divide up the world among the great imperialist states. Their strength becomes such that they become the power behind the scenes, and they exercise their influence over governments, especially in the policy of expansion and domination over colonies and undeveloped countries. When the imperialistic policy is terminated by there being no more lands to seize and suck dry, those states which have been late in the rush for colonization or left behind for some reason grow jealous of the countries which have had the best pickings, with the inevitable result of friction and war. Imperialism is, therefore, "the eve of the proletarian revolution."

Lenin's *The State and Revolution* was written in the

throes of the Russian revolution in 1917, and bears the marks of the experiences and the decisions of that time. He is insistent on the Marxist doctrine that the state, no matter how favorable to socialism it may appear, is of its nature an organ of the oppressors. No steps should be taken to collaborate with the state—what is needed is the dictatorship of the proletariat. This society of the people must take the place of the old state, and it can be brought about without too much difficulty by training the workers in the various trade and business organizations and turning them into bureaucrats. Not yet sufficiently experienced in the defects of a young proletariat he takes for granted that the beginnings of a perfect society are attained when the people freely take their part "in the everyday administration of affairs." Before his death he was to revise this opinion and to show an increasing distrust of the bureaucrat. At the time of the revolution he had had to make up his mind about the strategy he would follow. He was at loggerheads with the Russian Social-Democratic party with which he had collaborated when in exile in Switzerland. The Menshevists, as they came to be called, accepted the provisional Government after the fall of the Tsar. Neither the Menshevists nor the Bolshevists had previously believed in the real possibility of a Marxian régime in Russia. Both had interpreted the doctrine of Marx as meaning that industrialism was a necessary stage in the dialectic of societies. When Russia was defeated by Japan, Lenin had written that the war was nothing but a bourgeois incident and did not interest him: "To wish to attain socialism without passing through the stage of political democracy is merely to arrive at ridiculous and reactionary conclusions." In accordance with this doctrine the Menshevists did not plan for a socialist society; they assumed that the Provisional Government would inaugurate the bourgeois and industrial state which had to precede their final aim. They were ready therefore to work with the Provisional Government. Lenin, on the other hand, grasped the situation and straightway directed that there should be no collaboration with the acting government, but instead that they should act so as to give power to the Soviets, the land to the peasants and bring the war to an end.

The success of these tactics, however, left him with a gigantic task, the re-creation after the Marxist model of an enormous population of peasants and uneducated workers. It is no wonder that the idea of the "party" came to play such an essential role in his policies. The masses of the people, uneducated and disunited, were incapable of transforming themselves from a pre-industrial society into a socialist one. A spearhead was needed, which would be like religious under vows, utterly devoted and of one mind, organized and technically trained. Plekhanov, from whom Lenin had learnt so much in his earlier days, protested against this usurpation by the party of the part which the masses ought to play. Plekhanov fought a losing battle, though he could quote Marxist scripture for his view. The Russian experiment demanded a party, and the party became a consecrated élite which led the people through the bewildering struggles they had to face. The people had to be trained in the use of power and to be taught ruthlessly the iniquity of de-

viating from the one orthodoxy which would ultimately benefit them. Like the creation of Eve from the
body of Adam this formation of the party within Marxism was to have a momentous, and some would say, a
fatal impact on world history and the development of
the Communist system. Lenin claimed that only by
the party could the proletariat become conscious of its
own interests, and again only by the party's leadership
could theory and practice keep alongside one another.
There was constant danger of deviationism, of hereti-
cal thinking or action. He was ruthless in his resolve to
crush any such errors or forms of sabotage, and Stalin,
by his very genius in dealing with such situations, developed the party so that the party became a more
select party within the party, this select body yielded
to a central committee and the committee to one dictator. This centralization of power is the outstanding
feature of the Stalin régime, and though Stalin declared
that "There is dogmatic Marxism and creative Marxism; I take my stand on the second," the creations of
Stalin contribute little for a comparison of communism and Christianity in doctrine. Under his leadership, however, the contrasts and, according to certain
critics, the supposed resemblances with the Catholic
Church, have become more pointed. In the books written by refugees from Russia or by ex-Communists
it is common to find a bitter disappointment. The high
hopes and the ideals they entertained, they say, have
been betrayed in the totalitarian state fashioned by
Stalin. The stories which they tell of espionage and de-
lation, of trials and purges, of massacres, forcible deportations of peoples and concentration camps, have

scandalized and sickened many former sympathizers. "The true revolutionary is cold and unmerciful to mankind out of a kind of mathematical mercifulness. . . . A conscience renders one as unfit for the revolution as a double chin. Conscience eats through the brain like a cancer, until the whole of the grey matter is devoured." "Within the span of three generations," as Koestler says again in another place, "the Communist movement had traveled from the era of the Apostles to that of the Borgias."

To all such criticism Stalin has replied and quoted as on his side both Marx and Lenin. Marxism is realistic and its opponents are moved by bourgeois sentiment and bourgeois ethics. "The bourgeois democrats," says Lenin, "have always advanced and still advance all sorts of 'slogans in order to deceive the people. The point is to *test* their sincerity, to compare their words with their *deeds,* not to be satisfied with idealistic or charlatan *phrases,* but to get down to class *reality.'* " Those who are conscious of "class reality" cannot be sentimental. "The dictatorship of the proletariat is a most determined and most ruthless war waged by the new class against *a more powerful* enemy, the bourgeoisie, whose resistance is increased tenfold by its overthrow." "The dictatorship of the proletariat is a persistent struggle—sanguinary and bloodless, violent and peaceful, military and economic, educational and administrative—against the forces and traditions of the old society." So much for realism, and as for the rôle the party must play and for centralized power Lenin is at one with Stalin. "The dictatorship of the prole-tariat is a persistent struggle . . . the force of habit of millions and tens of millions is a most terrible force. Without an iron party tempered in the struggle, without a party enjoying the confidence of all that is honest in the given class, without a party capable of watching and influencing the mood of the masses, it is impossible to conduct such a struggle successfully." Hence says Stalin: "The Party could not have risen to so high an importance and could not have overshadowed all other forms of organization of the proletariat, if the latter were not confronted with the problem of power, if the conditions of imperialism, the inevitability of wars, and the existence of crises did not demand the concentration of all the forces of the proletariat at one point, the gathering of all the threads of the revolutionary movement into one spot in order to overthrow the bourgeoisie and to achieve the dictatorship of the proletariat. The proletariat needs the Party first of all as its General Staff, which it must have for the successful seizure of power. It need hardly be proved that without a Party capable of rallying around itself the mass organizations of the proletariat, and of centralizing the leadership of the entire movement during the progress of the struggle, the proletariat in Russia could never have established its revolutionary dictatorship."

Engaged in action as Lenin and Stalin have been, their language is bound to appear different from that of Marx, who had to compose his books at a desk in the British Museum. Marx had made a fundamental distinction between the sources of production and the superstructure of ideas which were determined by them. If we wish to know what man is and how he progresses and what determines his history, we must go and look at the changing economic conditions. Marx does not himself always observe the distinction he has made, and in the writings of Lenin and Stalin economics and politics become almost equipollent. Lenin was forced by concrete reality to advocate political action, and once he had emphasized the importance of the party political power assumed such an ascendancy that the forces of production are swallowed up in it. Plekhanov had reason to dispute the handing over of power to a party and the over-centralization which had to follow. Such a transference brought with it the obsession with politics and what to many seems the confusion of economics with politics. Moreover, for a party to have power is a contradiction of the first principle of Marxism, that socialism comes about by the transference of power for the first time in history to the people. All had gone wrong before and led to wrong and to oppression because a minority had possession of power. The power in the hands of a minority corrupts and leads dialectically to its opposite, and the party, no matter how much it may say that it is acting in the name of the masses—and most governments pretend the same—is in fact a minority, a minority which in time tends to hide the activities of one man.

Lenin's contribution is not confined to his concrete proposals to overcome the difficulties of his time. His keen mind saw that the materialistic philosophy and science of Marx needed to be brought up to date and made consistent with contemporary ideas. In this interest he is more indebted to Engels than to Marx, for Engels stayed longer over the philosophic problems than his friend and handed over the elements of a solution to succeeding Communist thinkers. With Marx he revolted against the Hegelian and objective idealism of the Germans. Nature is not the product of thought, but thought of nature. The old realist philosophers from Aristotle onwards would have agreed that thought did not make nature. Engels and Marx went further. They had in mind the idealists and declared the opposite of the idealists to be true. The result was that they write often of realism and materialism as if they were the same, as if, that is, there were no alternative to idealism save that of materialism. This special kind of realism was accepted by Lenin, and on its assumptions he had to consider the difficulties raised by the scientific theories of his time. Mechanical physics were the password in the days of Marx. Since then the atomic theory had undergone startling changes. The atom had ceased to be the ultimate unit of matter and the old material concepts were being so transformed, that the very existence of matter was raised in a new form. Scientists at a loss now to grasp the elusive structure of matter were turning more and more to a consideration of certain of its properties. Lenin, feeling that the ground was yielding under his feet, took the line in his *Materialism and Empiriocriticism* that all such purely scientific theories were of secondary importance. What concerned the philosopher was the objective character of matter. "According to philosophical materialism, the only property of matter that must necessarily be admitted is its character of objective reality—the fact that it exists outside our knowledge." This statement could be made with equal consistency by a realist like St. Thomas Aquinas and by a materialist, but it provided an alibi for his materialism if the physical scientists became too mischievous in their theories of matter.

One development in scientific theory was a godsend, namely, the attribution of movement to matter. The mechanical theory had not been so propitious, but now that matter was ever in change it could be made to include almost anything. The magic word transformation could be made to cover not only heat and light and chemical processes and electricity, but life and even spirit. Lenin and his successors felt that they had the right to replace mechanical change by qualitative change, and under this aspect of matter the emergence of quite new qualities could be justified. Furthermore, the justification could be formulated in terms of the dialectic of opposites. Within nature there is movement or change, and this means that reality is composed of elements which are opposed to each other like Hegel's being and non-being, and they are held together in a dialectical union, positive and negative, the continuous and the discontinuous, and so on in the different order of matter. Biology presents the same fusion of contradictories, life and death, and of course in society there is always present the same kind of struggle between classes. In this series of changes quantity changes into quality, physical matter, for instance, into living matter and living matter into conscious life. To make this theory fully in accord with historical materialism the Communist thinkers have been obliged to think of all these changes as occurring in time in the same sense in which human acts make history, and this is an extraordinary assumption which they have not been at pains to verify. The classless society, as we have seen, is to come at the end of a long history of struggle which has been divided by Marx into five principal periods. Here time is a determinant, but in what sense and with what truth can we speak of time as a determinant in the so-called qualitative change of oxygen and nitrogen into water or of similar changes in electricity?

Marx and Engels had derived consciousness from matter, but it was Lenin who worked out a philosophical theory of knowledge. It is called the "theory of reflection." That is to say, out of matter the brain develops, and at a sufficiently developed stage of brain development the organism acquires the property of perceiving the processes within itself and reflecting them. The physical process and the perception are not to be thought of as two different realities; they are rather two aspects of the same thing, what has been named the "theory of the two sides" or two aspects. This perception, since it is only the other side of the physical object, is said to be an image of it and to represent it faithfully. By this means Lenin hopes to give the physical reality priority and at the same time to assure himself and his fellow materialists that they are saying what is true. The Marxist doctrine has to be true and at the same time to be the outcome of materialistic principles. He goes further and tries to show that the usual dialectic of opposites is illustrated in his theory of knowledge. The "thing in itself" has to become the "thing for us," but not in the idealist fashion of Hegel who reconciled the object, the estranged self, with the idea or the subjective self. Lenin, on the contrary, argues that the physical processes are transformed into subjective ones, first into the sensible perception and then by another transformation of a dialectical character into abstract thinking, but throughout the transformation of quantity into quality and quality into perception and thought it is the matter, the determining laws of external reality, which control and constitute the dialectic.

As Marxism developed, and after the revolution became a world force, the need of keeping it on orthodox lines became more and more imperative. This is the reason why the writings of Lenin and Stalin are full of savage criticism of those who within the ranks dared to differ from them. Stalin, for instance, interposed in the disputes about the relation of science to Marxism. The solution offered by Lenin and some of his disciples had not laid the ghost of idealism or of mechanical science. Lenin belabored those whom he called Menshevist idealists as well as the upholders of the old mechanical materialism, and at the same time he permitted the philosophers, who held that Marxism was a genuine and world philosophy, to continue their teaching The same extreme sensitiveness to deviationism is seen in the well-known dispute over the theories of Lysenko. What has come out of these disputes is that communism must be regarded and treated as a crusading and revolutionary philosophy and possessing a rigid orthodoxy. As Stalin declared: "Of all our party's heritage, the most important and richest legacy is its ideological asset, its basic direction, its revolutionary standpoint."

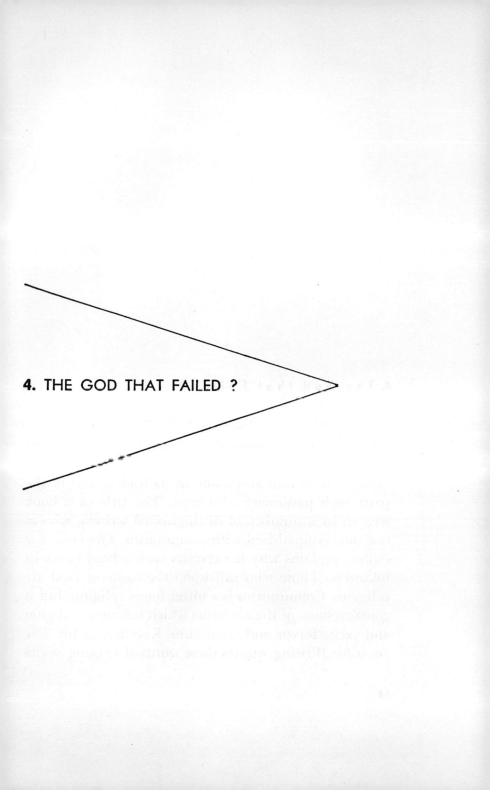

4. THE GOD THAT FAILED ?

4. The God that Failed?

The account of communism given in the preceding chapters does not explain fully why it has drawn so many into its fold and made of its leaders and of the party such passionate adherents. The title of a book written by a number of distinguished writers, who at one time sympathized with communism, *The God that Failed,* explains why it exercises such a hold upon its followers. Those who call upon the name of God are religious. Communism is a bitter foe of religion, but it contains some of the elements which belong to religion and excite fervor and fanaticism. Koestler, in his *The Invisible Writing,* quotes these words of a young Soviet official. "We are believers. Not as you are. We do not believe either in God or in men. We manufacture gods and we transform men. We believe in Order. We will create a universe in our image, without weaknesses, a universe in which man, rid of the old rags of Christianity, will attain his cosmic grandeur, in the supreme culmination of the species. We are not fighting for a régime, or for power, or for riches. We are the instruments of Fate."

What is most noticeable about this declaration of faith is its optimism and its youthful optimism. The words would not be in character if purporting to come from Lenin in his latter days or from Stalin. They represent the passionate reaction to the imagined lying humbug of the creeds, which he thinks have outlasted their day and are nothing but rags. "The gods like great black oxen tread the world, and I am broken by their passing feet." No matter what the orator in the pulpit or on the platform said, the world was becoming more and more intolerable and inhuman. In Marx's lifetime the enemy was idealism of which the archangel was Hegel, and by idealism the Communists meant all that false optimism, the vaporous sentimentalism, the substitution of religious and theoretical ideals for reality. Now optimism has changed to a despairing attitude and in our modern society the old beliefs when retailed too often look deformed or gangrenous. The world is closing in upon man and he is offered communism as the one means of struggling with it and bestriding it. Critics of Marxism say of it that it is a gross simplification of life; but this criticism fails of its effect at a time when many men are uncertain and muddled in their motives, and longing for simplifications. Those of divided will succumb readily to a commanding personality or a commanding and terse creed. Such a creed has the advantages of a map and compass in a strange and desert land. I call it a creed because without a doubt it drew many into its fold not as a scientific prediction or program but as a crusade bringing salvation to the oppressed and offering a certain solution to the problems of society. The combination of science and prophecy is one of the outstanding features of Marxism. We shall have to ask later whether this combination is a possible one, but it is unquestionable that not only Marx, but Lenin and Stalin also, spoke and acted as if inspired; and the tomb of Lenin in the Red Square by the Kremlin in Moscow bears witness to the impression which the party wished to create.

The fact that Marx and Engels argued that religion once served a purpose and that now communism had superseded it gives a warrant for holding that some of the motive power contained in religion must be present in communism. But whereas communism is the dialectical synthesis of preceding political and social ideas—and Marx could admit the virtues of a past bourgeois society—no true communist calls the same tune for religion. It is to be given no quarter. It is the first enemy to be destroyed. Marx, in his examination of Hegel's *Philosophy of Right,* does call religion the "opium of the people," and he explains what he means. The people in past ages lived in a world of oppression and unhappiness, and, therefore, they created for themselves an illusory world of happiness to which they could retreat. In so far as religion gave some crumbs of comfort it did good, but now when the people can achieve real happiness such illusion is not only a distraction but a fatal narcotic. How contemptuously Lenin thought of religion is shown by such words as: "The impotence of the exploited classes in their struggle with their exploiters engenders faith in a better life hereafter, just as inevitably as the impotence of the savage in his struggle with nature engenders faith in gods, demons, and prodigies."

A conversation with Socrates, even with Marcus Aurelius, would quickly have disabused Lenin and dispelled Marx's airy generalizations about religion. Marx was a baptized Jew, but the milieu in which he was brought up was not favorable to religion. Christianity was at a low ebb at the time, and the ideas of the Enlightenment widespread. The age of Reason had guillotined religion as well as the French royalty, and the ideas of Voltaire and Fichte permeated the atmosphere. The younger Hegel had adapted the Christian language of sin and atonement to his dialectic and the terms he used, estrangement and reconciliation, reappear in Marx. But Marx, from all the evidence we have, knew very little at first hand of Christian theology. What is more likely is that the undying hopes of Jewry in the advent of a Messiah and the kingdom of Israel influenced consciously or unconsciously his mind. Christopher Dawson and other writers have remarked on the curious parallels between the vision of Marx and that of the Jewish people in the Old Testament. In both, the oppressions and struggles of the time were to be succeeded by a period of righteousness, by a kingdom of plenty and of peace. Marx, a Jew by race and a

Christian for form's sake, had all the thwarted impulses of the ghetto and hatred of the smug superiority of the Gentile surviving in him. His break with the Jewish community and religion and admission into bourgeois society denied him the Jewish Messianic vision, but it could not prevent him from detesting the current bourgeois attitude. The idealism of the time into which his potential apocalyptic longing was diverted looked to him little more than empty bourgeois sentiment. All his attention, therefore, was turned on the life around him, to the heartless conditions of the poor and the grievances of the workers, and he traced the sources of them to the love of cupidity, inherent in a capitalist society. He stripped away the mantle of idealism and exposed the false claims of the liberals and idealists to be the children of the enlightenment. In this perspective the bourgeois, as Christopher Dawson suggests, took the place of the Gentile, and the economic poor, the proletariat, took the place of the spiritual poor of the Bible. The result was paradoxical, if not a combination of opposites. Into the cold logic of his theory of material determinism and of the necessary conflict of classes burst the old moral and spiritual passion transforming the theory into a revolutionary crusade, which would end once and for all—let the dialectic be what it may—the long oppression of God's poor and the ages of injustice, the reign of the city of avarice and strife. Thus by the principle of strife he would end strife, and by determinism bring freedom, and by materialism create the kingdom of the spirit which Israel had been promised.

Whatever be thought of this interpretation of the

messianic element in Marx, the similarity of his vision to that of the Old Testament is striking, and it makes the task of comparing the system with that of a religion like Christianity relatively easy. So easy, indeed, does the comparison appear that many have been beguiled into making a treaty between the two or accepting communism as a form of religion superior to that of Christianity. D. F. Buxton in *The Challenge of Bolshevism* argues that the Communists provided by their example the Christianity which the bourgeois Christian society preached but did not practice. R. Crossman, again, tells us that the intellectual who becomes a Communist feels "the prickings of his Christian conscience far more acutely than many of his unreflective Church-going neighbors." Silone, to take one more instance, tells us that where he was born and brought up, "the ashes of skepticism have never suffocated, in the hearts of those who suffered most, the ancient hope of the kingdom of God on earth, the old expectation of charity taking the place of law . . ." and his motive for becoming a Communist was that as a member he thought that he would be helping in the attainment of these hopes. These and others sought in place of Christianity what they thought a more alive faith.

Others have stayed Christians in intention, but felt that there was much to learn from Marxism and wished therefore for some kind of alliance. To the degree that Christianity reassesses and reinforces itself with the best in every culture without detriment to its creed, all Christians should look for whatever is of permanent value in communism. But the writers of whom I am thinking go further. They regard communism as having something both religious and vital which Christianity cannot afford to neglect. (I will leave aside those who are to all intents and purposes Communists but add the prefix "Christian" perhaps to signify that they are religious at heart.) In England, Professor J. Macmurray is the protagonist of those who foresee a new and genuine Christianity in the dialectical meeting of Marxism and "official Christianity." Marxism has the virtues, he thinks, of the old Judaic religion. It takes this world seriously and works to the establishment of the common people here upon earth. Like the Judaic religion it looks to the kingdom of God upon earth, and has no use for a far off transcendent divine event. Preoccupied, however, with the dialectical struggle, it has so far no room for God or for what Christianity has to offer as its special gift. Christianity affirms the rule of God and the law of love, but in fact it is suffocated by worldliness and by its identification with bourgeois interests. To live and propagate its essential gospel, namely that of love and the society of persons in fellowship, it must unite itself with the one force which is in fact bringing about this new society. Marxism, on the other hand, by restricting itself to one party of society, large as it undoubtedly is, fails in its universal appeal and in what should be its aim, namely, the regeneration of the whole of human society. It fails, too, by relying entirely on the materialistic forces of production. It must find room for God and the true expression of God, that charity which is made concrete in the mutual love of persons. The dialectic of opposites invites this union as the failings of both sides would be eliminated, and the result would be pure gain.

One of the most distinguished Protestant theologians, Paul Tillich, also believes that Christianity has something to learn from Marx. He tells us that his relation with Karl Marx "has always been dialectical, combining a Yes and a No. The Yes was based on the prophetic, humanistic, and realistic element in Marx's passionate style and profound thought, the No on the calculating, materialistic, and resentful elements in Marx's analysis, polemic and propaganda." He is not disturbed by the explicitly atheistic philosophy of Marx because he thinks that while it is atheist in conscious intention it is religious in essence. It is fighting the evil in contemporary Christianity, namely the Pharisaism and legalism. "Religion reflects, in the imperfect way accessible to the limited mind of man, the structure of the universe and man's place in it." In this sense of religion Marx is considered highly religious, and right, too, in uniting all theory with practice. Man is on the march to his destiny, and a genuine religious philosophy must take man as a whole, as a thinking, desiring and active being, as one in mind and body. Marx, therefore, is on the right lines in fixing on the material forces of production as the prime mover in the historical development of man; and he is consistent and sensible in distinguishing between the real material structure of society and the superstructure or ideology men build upon the existing economic conditions. We are idealists if we separate man's thought from the determining influences of life, just as we are again if we erect a notion of freedom which is not a knowledge of our fixed destiny. Where Tillich differs from Marx is in his interpretation of the dialectic of man. Marx is so obsessed by his materialistic explanation that he forgets the high meaning he has given to man's work and struggle. Instead of the prophetic insight into the value of the dialectic as signifying the transformation of man at the ripe moments of history, the coming together of the absolute and the temporal, a future time is foreseen when all will be well and the dialectic will cease to function. This classless society Tillich terms utopianism.

The reaction of Tillich, Macmurray, Dean Hewlett Johnson and so many others is evidence of the religious appeal which communism can make, and it explains, too, in what sense it can be called a religion or a substitute for religion. But it must be added that much depends upon the truth of the interpretation of it, and as touching the Christian religion, what version of Christianity the interpreters may have in mind. Macmurray, for instance, writes as if nothing in Christianity were of lasting value and truth except charity, which he identifies with "friendship-relations" and a society of "persons in fellowship." But friendship is not peculiar to Christianity. It is the aim of Freemasons and Rotarians as well as of Quakers. Tillich, on the other hand, is certainly Christian in that he exalts God before all and centers all endeavor and all history in Christ. But his view is a very personal one which develops very freely at times entirely from the hitherto generally accepted Christian faith. He departs from the traditional doctrine of the supernatural, that is, the ancient teaching about grace and otherworldliness; he does not seem to accept the doctrine about the nature and person of Christ defined in the great councils of the

Church, nor again the idea of a Church which teaches with authority in the name of Christ.

Anyone is free to form his own view of what Christianity is even after nineteen hundred years of its existence. But such a person, who must believe on his own premises that Christ's teaching has been misunderstood for so long, must also have a very different idea of the sacredness and authority of Christ from that which has been taught from apostolic times. A Revelation, which professes to be direct from God and for all mankind, ought not to have to wait nineteen hundred years to be decoded rightly. In other words, a Christianity which has been misunderstood and in error for so long, reflects upon the wisdom and authority of its Founder. Just because of this it would not be fitting in a book such as this to contrast communism as a faith with some new interpretation of Christianity, however interesting. In men's minds Christianity stands vaguely no doubt but finally for that religion and philosophy of life which has kept a unity and consistency down the ages and influenced the thought and aspirations of every generation. It is this perennial, as it may be called, Christianity which stands up still as the competitor in the field with communism. But as this perennial or orthodox Christian faith is so vaguely understood, it will be necessary to give a sketch of it, emphasizing the points where it encounters the doctrines of communism.

Tillich, as we have seen, regards part of the teaching of Marx as true, and there are others who agree with this view. Now Marx can be looked at as a scientist, a historian, a political thinker, and as a philosopher. No matter how uncompromisingly orthodox a Christian may be, there is no antecedent reason why he should not learn from the science or historical conclusions of Marx. With the advance in the sciences there must always be something new to learn and probably something out of date to forget. Whether Marx has added to human knowledge is a question of fact. Philosophy is somewhat different, as a philosophy usually deals with ultimates and its parts are closely interconnected in a general outlook on life. That this is so in Marx is claimed by Lenin in words which I have already quoted. The fierce opposition to any form of revisionism confirms this, and all the chief Communist writers confirm this. As Leonov says: "Bolshevism's treasury of ideas is something the Party guards as the apple of its eye. The unshakable foundation of this possession is our Party's idea of the world, dialectical materialism." The stray ideas, therefore, of other philosophers may perhaps be appropriated—though it usually happens that when this is done, being out of their context they are misunderstood—but Marx is inviolable. Tillich, and indeed, Macmurray, believe that if the Marxian vision of society be improved by a better understanding of man and God's relation with man or by more human fellowship, his insight into the dialectic of history can be pronounced truly Christian. Tillich thinks that Marxism favors the individual and personal freedom and actually in 1934 said that in Russia the aim "is not the state but the individual and the full development of his collectivistic activities." That Russia has any such intentions is more than doubtful to judge from the evidence of its policies and acts or from the writings of Marx. Russia putting theory into practice builds vast dams and industrial works and forces collective farming on a peasant community, the theory being that man is materialistic and the product of economic forces. This has been called "a universal mechanism of calculable processes," and granted that this is offset by a human wish to improve the condition of the workers, the view of man contained in it is far removed from the Christian emphasis on person and the ideal of personal freedom.

But although the Marxist and the Christian estimate of the human person differs, we have still to consider which is true. Too many rush to adopt Marxist ideas without examining what they mean or how far they can stand up to criticism. The truth is, I think, that Marx, outside the field of economics, was not an expert, and as a result his system may be rich in suggestion, but it is full of loose thinking. Lenin says of it: "The Marxian doctrine is omnipotent because it is true. It is complete and harmonious, and provides men with an integral world conception which is irreconcilable with any form of superstition, reaction, or defence of bourgeois oppression." This is a high claim. It means that Marx has said the last word on "dialectic," on "materialism," and on the nature of man and of history. Nevertheless it is almost impossible to get a clear and consistent idea of what Marx meant by Materialism. It is the opposite of the Hegelian idealism. Hegel held that material reality was only an externalization of the mind, and therefore ultimately thought must be the sole reality. The opposite of this is realism, that is to say, the view that mind does not make things. Such a view is quite compatible with holding that mind and matter, spirit and body, however closely united, nevertheless belong to two different orders. This is probably the commonsense view and the most widely held one. In some places it would look as if Marx meant no more than this, and later, when Lenin was embarrassed by the new views of the physical scientists on matter, he explicitly says that "according to philosophical materialism, the only property of matter that must necessarily be admitted is its character of objective reality—the fact that it exists outside our knowledge." On such a definition materialism is another word for realism. But undoubtedly all Marxists have an antipathy to allowing the existence of anything which cannot be explained in terms of physical nature, and conveniently the new dialectical process could be used to clear up all mysteries. Hence human activities are not contrasted with material movements; they are merely a development of it, life developing from the inanimate, and the human from the animal. Animal subsistence reaches a higher level with the use of tools and from thenceforward the growths and struggles of societies are made dependent, like the hands of a watch on its works, on the forces of production. What is material is the structure; the superstructure of legal, political, and moral ideas is determined by this structure. Similarly in Lenin's theory of knowledge there is an attempt to explain the mind's activities and concepts as issuing from what is material. The realist would say that through impressions on the senses the mind is given content and stimulus; that is enough to refute the idealist contention.

But Lenin reduces thought to sense and sense to another aspect of matter. Thought becomes a property of matter, the inside of what is outside, that is, the physical reality. He speaks too of "images" and "copies" and "reflections." Such a view is an echo of Hume's empiricism without any of the subtlety and plausibility of the latter. It is impossible to think of a universal idea or what at times is called a "logical construction" as simply a material image. An image is as particular as the object it images, and if we take refuge in a composite image we are still far from what we mean when we use a concept like triangle or reason.

Moreover Marx and Lenin suppose that there is a superstructure of ideas, political and moral and legal. In so far as these ideas may be influenced by the economic conditions, and I would add ideas of the time, the Communist view can bring much evidence in its support; but what meaning can we attach to the statement that the political and the moral ideas are nothing more than the inside aspect of the external processes of production, that they are an image as a face in a mirror is an image of the person looking into it? Nor can it be said in answer that the image need not be so exact a replica, for if this line be taken then the whole virtue of the materialistic argument is lost. We are changing our premises and covertly introducing a new idea which is not contained in what we know of matter. Throughout the Marxist system there is this hidden angel of spirit joining together what is not on materialist principles joined, and covering up defects. An animal using a tool is converted into a man who does more by his freedom and the ingenuity of his mind to create a new life for himself than can be explained by the simple words that an animal uses a tool. In the dialectics of history as it moves onwards from primitive man, there is presupposed throughout a direction and moral improvement which makes no sense unless an elixir be added to the brew concocted out of material elements. I defy anyone to explain from purely material counters how and why there should be this gradual enlightenment of man culminating in a system of thought and action which will prelude and produce a truth—the Marxist system—which is not subject to any change, which must not be revised, which is itself pertinent and applicable at a time when the forces of production and the economic situation will be different from what it is now. Truth on Marxian principles is part of the superstructure determined by the structure of the material forces of the time, and as an ideology its value is relative and changing. The Marxist aware of this weakness declares that whereas the capitalist theories are subjectivist and created for their own benefit, his own theories are objectivist. They are identical with the objective reality, and are the expression of the proletariat's knowledge of necessity and of the objective needs of humanity. Reality and knowledge, therefore, here meet. But apart from the vagueness of such expressions as "objective needs of humanity," which look very question-begging, the Communist still has to show that his very statement of the answer escapes from being an ideology. He has to lift himself up by his own bootstraps above the subjective and relative, when by his own theory or rather by the necessity of physical conditions he is bound to be subjective.

In pronouncing in favor of matter as the one ground of all that exists, the Marxist is forced to reduce thought, imagination, morals and religion to a materialistic level. The means which he uses to maintain this truth and to keep up the prestige of ideas, social, artistic, and moral is the dialectic. Matter is in movement and moves upward by the collision of opposites and the consequent emergence of something qualitatively new. This law is made to serve as an explanation of the emergence of life from the non-living and of the human from the animal and the thinking activity from the animal activity. Now no evidence so far has been found to prove the emergence of the living from the non-living. It is a scientific hypothesis waiting confirmation. Marx took science seriously and asked that what he wrote should be treated as a work of science. Nevertheless, he here goes beyond the claims of science and lays down as a necessary and obvious truth of his system what the scientist regards as a hypothesis. He feels justified in being so dogmatic on an undecided question of fact because the dialectic demands it. The dialectic is called in and exercises powers which excel those of the genie of Aladdin's lamp. This is neither science nor philosophy. A word which has a similar prestige and a somewhat similar function is "evolution," and the theory of evolution in Marx's lifetime became popular and served to fortify his dialectical materialism. But evolution is another case in point of a hypothesis which can be used with exactness and also with such indefiniteness as to lose significance. As applied to the gradual development of species it has, since the days of Lamarck and Darwin and Weismann, reached greater and greater precision. But there is no such precision when evolution is extended to the evolution of the stars or the evolution of thought or religion.

Dialectic, as already noted, was used with sufficient precision by the Greeks to describe knowledge obtained in the exchange of apparently conflicting views. The discussion brought out the fact that for the most part the ideas held by each disputant were narrow-minded and partial and were advanced and widened by this interchange and conflict. Hence came the theory that, by this means of dialectic, knowledge could be constantly improved and perfected so as finally to arrive at full truth. Hegel exploited this method of knowledge, and certainly showed that this dialectic was a natural human way of advancing in learning. Unfortunately as an idealist he extended what is a human and imperfect way of knowing to all reality. Dialectic became as essential to every realm of reality, the physical, the animal, and the human world, history, religion, and metaphysics, as breathing in and out is essential to the life of the body. Reality, in fact, is revealed to us as behaving dialectically. In applying this key-idea Hegel composed a vast work of genius, full of insights and follies. He tried to forestall the scientist and the historian in his explanation of natural and historical events, with the result that this part of his work is out of date and covered with fungus. To watch him forcing everything into the flow and ebb of the dialectic is a lesson in wisdom, but not that of Solomon. Being, for instance, has to be opposed by non-being, and out of this comes becoming. Mind is one, but it has to splinter and become its opposite dark nature, which in turn comes back to being mind in a synthesis of the two. The self is the self and almost empty unless it has its opposite "the other," and out of this comes the community, but, be it noted, the real problem here is how the self should not lose its selfhood in a unity with other selves. God is being itself, but goes out from himself into the process of human minds. He is immanent in this process and all human minds and human thinking is in the end declared to be within the divine and final synthesis. I give these various examples to show the diversity of application of the dialectical principle, and the difficulty of applying it universally.

Marx, while he rejected the idealism of Hegel, kept the principle of the dialectic, and he involved himself in all the same kinds of difficulties. Even on the chosen ground of human thinking, where it has most precision, it is not the only way in which thinking operates and knowledge grows. We benefit from hearing other points of view, but some of them we may reject utterly as false, others we may assimilate as fitting in with and complementing our own viewpoint, whilst others again we may resist, struggle with, but finally select from, to the correction and improvement of our original view. This latter alone is the synthesis of apparently conflicting views and therefore dialectical in character. When we turn to the advances in physical and chemical science in the last hundred years or to the improvements in medicine and chemistry only the thinker with an *idée fixe* would subsume them all under the heading of dialectic. Each branch of knowledge has its own methods and technique, and the higher we go the less are we certain of any rule which can do justice to the variations confronting us. Just for this reason bad philosophers longing by hook or by crook to introduce order into the recalcitrant material produce a formula or a yardstick. The simplicity of the formula tempts many for a time, and it is true that many an inadequate formula has served indirectly to promote knowledge. The Greek theory of numbers, the ancient atomism, the four humors, Yin and Yang, the vital force, utilitarianism and natural selection, each of these at different times and in various fields has been a fashionable formula of this kind, and I am afraid that the dialectical process belongs to this family.

In a world of change and growth where there is unity and multiple diversity it is always possible to fix on one kind of change and make out a case for its dialectical features. Marx did a service to economic history by pointing to certain recurring features in it which had not been fully recognized. With the help of this suggestion economic experts have been led to examine them more closely and to draw some probable conclusions. Moreover Marx has undoubtedly shown that the forces of production do play a more important role in historical development than had been suspected, and that the legal, literary and political ideas of successive epochs have been affected by them. Once seen, this truth becomes obvious, but the credit is to Marx for having been the first to elicit it clearly and prove it. But when this influence is made paramount, and when the so-called dialectic process in economic change is so extended as to cover all human history, the theory gives more darkness than light. It does not follow, for instance, that men after discovering the usefulness of tools should oppose each other and split into classes. Unless power corrupts and unless avarice be stronger than good fellowship, a division of labor may lead to equitableness and friendship. In a family the division of labor is usually a happy one. And as society grows the possible alternatives in development spread and multiply. Seldom can we say in looking at history that such and such a course was inevitable and predictable in detail. Neither in its Edo period (1615–1868) nor in its Meiji (1868–1912) does Japanese history conform to the Marxist pattern; nor does the story of the Reductions of Paraguay, nor indeed do the developments in England since the death of Marx. Even of what has happened in Russia itself Raymond Aron can write: "But during recent decades there has been an ever widening gap between the ideology and the event, between Marxist theories and reality. It is obvious, in retrospect, that the Russian Revolution of 1917 was nothing like the uprising of the Proletariat against Capitalism which Marx dreamed of as the supreme moment in human history. And 'the revolution from above' which prepared the way for Russian occupation of Eastern Europe cannot be assimilated to the vision of the self-destruction of the capitalist system, victim of its own contradictions." What has happened in history falls just as plausibly under some general theory of power, derived shall we say, from Hobbes or even Thrasymachus. A follower of such a view would have an excellent example, for instance, in the actions and policies of the Bolshevists. Country after country has been subjugated and turned into a vassal of Russia by a technique of power, a technique which enables a handful of men with a tiny minority of fellow travelers to occupy key positions and then to impose their will on the majority by the murder and deportation of their opponents' leaders. As Mr. Hugh Seton-Watson has said: "Stalin . . . may have been a coarser, crueler, and viler man than Lenin or Trotsky. But it was not this that was decisive. Give absolute power over a vast and backward nation to a tightly disciplined clique of professional revolutionaries who claim to possess the final scientific truth about human society, who regard men and women as clay to be molded to the purposes of History, and who have consciously abandoned, in practice as well as in theory, all absolute moral standards, and you can get only one result—totalitarianism. Whether the leader's name is Ulyanov or Bronstein or Djugashvili matters a good deal less."

These large-scale theories and patterns of history are stimulating to the mind because they provide that unity which we all crave. They are, however, anathema to the professional historian, because they are bound to ignore what is peculiar and proper to every phase of history. As in the joke, when asked to write on the elephant the Englishman tells of shooting one, the Frenchman of its amours, the German gives its phenomenological attributes, the Marxist would contrast it with a tractor and emphasize the class struggle of the sahib and the native, but the historian would give us accurate information about it and its relation to man. The Marxist claims to be infallible; he knows beforehand what must happen in the future, whereas the historian is content to find out what really happened in the past and what were the main reasons and causes why such and such events occurred and not others; as to the future he is slow to prophesy. Owing to the nature of his subject matter he does not, like the physical scientist, make prediction the test of his success. The Marxist, on the other hand, does pretend to predict, because he believes that in the materialist setting there is no difference between human affairs and physical phenomena.

It is the boast of Marx that he is the first to overcome the old uncertainties about history and the tentative methods used. History can be shown to be of the same order as the physical sciences and to be equally determined. Such a claim carries with it the duty of making predictions of what must happen in the future, and the Marxists are not chary of making them. But what they have foretold has been more like a prophecy than a prediction, and indeed the critics of Marx have accused him of unconsciously trying to be both prophet and scientist. One might add historian as well, since to most historians history is neither prophecy nor on all fours with the physical sciences. The critics point out that a scientific prediction has no shades; it says precisely when and how something must happen. When a Comet plane crashes the scientists seek to find out the exact causes and then so to improve the plane that it will with certainty withstand particular exterior and interior jolts and pressures. The weather prophets are called prophets just because they are not yet in a position to predict exactly what the weather in a certain place will be like in twelve hours. There are some generalized conclusions from experience which are more or less prophetic, such as that every cloud has a silver lining or that sin brings suffering and suffering wisdom. That truth is strong and will prevail is to a theist certain, but not to a pessimist. Now the Marxist is sure that truth, his truth, will prevail; he is also sure that this truth will be exhibited in the perfect classless society after the proletariat has taken power and the state has withered away. He professes to know this with scientific certainty, and he is led to say this by his belief that history can be put on the same basis as physics and chemistry. But his large scale calculations can never compare with the accurate small scale calculations of the chemist or electrician, and he resembles far more the prophet or seer who utters oracles which can be made to look right no matter what happens. Aristotle said the last word on human actions when he declared that judgment about them could hold only "for the most part." Large scale predictions may well come out in the long run, and the reason why is not far to seek. Human nature is sufficiently a constant to allow us to foretell that hunger and want, easy conditions, opportunities for power and ease will beget the same kinds of trouble in nations within an appreciable period of time. But history also shows that there are exceptions, as well as delays and diversions which no one can predict.

These and other weaknesses in Marxism follow from the oversimplification necessitated by the initial postulate. Idealism tried to reduce everything to the idea. Turn it upside down, and the answer is there in materialism. Committed to materialism the Communist is forced to reduce every type of experience and everything known to matter. But as all facts and all experiences cannot be forced into the mold of physical matter, the Marxian enlarges his definition of matter so as to include what is apparently very different from it. Such definitions are bound to be only nominal; the thought of butter or the longing and actual butter remain just as different as before, no matter whether they are called by the same name. But the Marxist does make a half-hearted attempt to show how they are interconnected and how it is that thought and desire have the same roots as the pumpkin and the pump. Matter is in movement and new qualities emerge in the dialectical process. But this only covers a mystery with words and prevents the Marxist from tackling the problem fairly and squarely. For instance, he tells us that freedom is the knowledge of necessity and goes on to speak of the mastery and direction of nature's laws by the true Communists, that is to say, by those who have realized this kind of freedom. This idea of freedom is borrowed from Hegel, and in Hegelianism the idea has much to commend it. It is akin to the religious ideal of identifying oneself with the will of God. But how can a materialist take over this sense without deserting his principles? Not only does the act of will consist in the identification of oneself with necessity, which is not the same as "knowledge," but the Marxist supposes that this knowledge includes the power to direct nature and its laws. Such a freedom goes far beyond what materialist principles can allow. In the same way Lenin assumes that by calling thought the other side of the external and the material, by limiting it again to being an image or reflection of the physical processes, he has managed to explain on material premises the whole world of ideas. But in what sense can the system of philosophy of Plato, the metaphysics of Plotinus, be called the other side or aspect of physical processes or just a reflection of them? (A play on the word "reflection" as meaning both a mirroring and a meditation cannot be meant.) And if metaphysics be an aspect, the other side of physical changes, the same must be also said of Dante's *Divine Comedy* and Marx's *Das Kapital*. Materialism has deprived itself of the wherewithal to give a proper account of the infinitely variegated universe; it is as if a plumber with his bag of tools were commissioned to make another city of Troy.

This criticism is necessary if we are to see Marxism in its proper proportions, and it is quite compatible with a respect for communism and with the belief that it holds out, however imperfectly, more promise for the future of society than any other system. The orthodox Marxists do not admit that their system needs revision, but other beliefs have been equally hotheaded in crediting all perfection to their creed and have in time modified and corrected the weaknesses. Communists have drawn hosts of men and women into their fold, and from every rank and every degree of culture. They claim that they offer the one means to human welfare which has been long sought for and never found. According to the canonical scriptures of Marxism men and women in former days having no prospect whatsoever of happiness on earth sought it in the imaginary world, in the myths of religion which guaranteed a life elsewhere of bliss. As society has developed and the workers have become more conscious of their rights religion has steadily been losing its hold, and the hope of a full human life has awakened. Various utopias have been described, utopias, because, though the vision was an earthly one, the ideal was unsubstantial and incapable of realization. Religion could not help because it was of its nature unworldly and in so far as it interested itself in this world it was servile to the powers that be. Liberalism was rooted in bad economics and was a creation of the few, the bourgeois. It fostered the idea of infinite progress and of a coming federation of man, but it served a class at the expense of the proletariat, and from its principles could issue not prosperity but economic and international crises. The resultant wars are to be attributed to the strains caused by bourgeois economic policies, which of their very nature perpetuate conflict. With such a comment constantly reiterated in a situation which is cloudy enough of itself to darken hopes, the Communist voice is like to that of one crying in the desert and announcing good news. The kingdom of heaven becomes the kingdom of this earth and answers to the expectations of the multitudes who have turned their minds from a religious prospect to a social and economic beatitude. Never before has a philosophy identified itself with action, and in setting itself up as a movement of the workers of the world. It has provided a program which boasts of being philosophically true, scientifically up to date and economically sound—and at the same time clear.

The lure, therefore, of an earthly paradise was offered at a time when men's minds were hankering after it and had been disappointed by the results of the

French Revolution. Those in authority frightened by the excesses of a revolutionary populace had recourse to methods of repression or to doling out freedom in driblets. As the nineteenth century advanced the liberal philosophers took on the role of emancipators, but their views like a boomerang hit and destroyed their own positions. The general feeling grew that the people must themselves take charge of their own welfare, and the sense of embattled union developed. The second word of the rallying cry of the French Revolution, fraternity, though it has little basis in the current philosophies, was the most moving emotionally. Communism has a winning aspect as the emblem of fraternity, and as the one force which can make it come alive. Moreover the poverty of so many millions, the distressing conditions of remuneration, of housing and health, which could be attributed to cutthroat competition and the indifference of the rich, stirred the generous minded and made them overlook possible defects in Marxism because of its zeal against the exploitation of the poor and its redemption of them in one fraternal society. Many had guilty consciences and so were won over to support the Communist party. Their motives were moral and at least indirectly religious, in that the feeling for justice and desire for brotherhood were implanted in the west by the Sermon on the Mount.

More philosophical, but equally strong, is the desire for co-ordination and unity in one's thoughts and actions. The question "why" is ever on the lips of the very young, and as we grow up we try to make sense of, that is, give a meaning to, our experiences. The more we learn the less easy is it to do this, and now that the fields of learning are so many and often so remote from one another, the mind is teased with the untidiness of its possessions. It is like a room in which there is complete disorder. This is one of the reasons why the middle-aged and the old cling to their prejudices or to views against all the evidence. The young like short cuts, formulas which give the answers, and they hasten after a teacher who provides the key to life's mysteries. This unity is too often a will of the wisp, and the charlatan or alchemist can put his spell on those who have lost their way. The mystic has his unity, but he is rare, and he is followed from a distance by the Blakes and a Yeats who wrote: "Nothing is an isolated artistic moment; there is a unity everywhere; everything fulfils a purpose that is not its own; the hailstone is a journeyman of God; the grass blade carries the universe upon its point." The great philosopher, too, succeeds, like Aristotle, in giving an intelligible unity to all that is, or attempts, like Whitehead, to do so. The trouble of the lesser thinkers is that they leave out so much or force reality to fit their Procrustean bed. The Communist comes upon the stage at a time when there is a desperate need for a vision, for a reassembling of the many new discoveries in terms of truth and purpose. His manifesto is not only a complete theory but also dynamic. It claims to have the answer to all the questions, to be armed *cap à pie* in philosophy, in science, in economics, and in its knowledge of man. It has nothing obscurantist or mystifying about it; it is authoritative and clear and, what is most attractive of all, it can be so mastered that with a few formulas the disciple can grapple and master any problem proposed to him.

It is not a matter of wonder, then, that it has succeeded beyond any of its rivals, and that to-day it is the most serious competitor to the Christianity which has up to now been the greatest influence in the Western world.

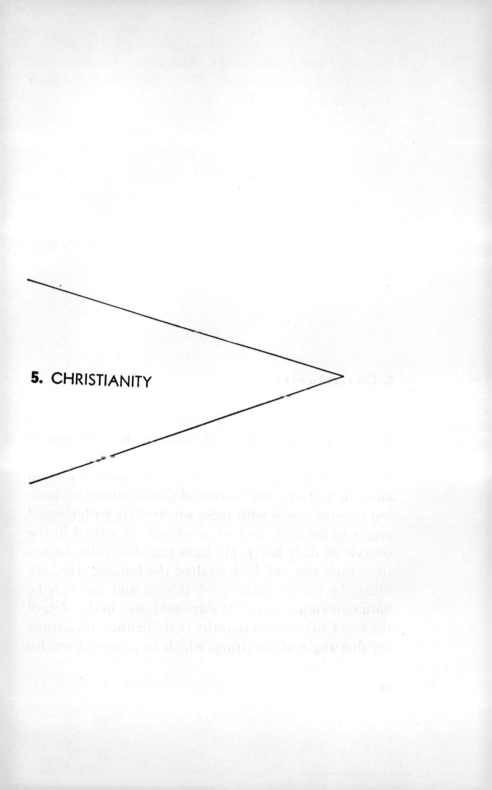

5. CHRISTIANITY

5. Christianity

For one engrossed in social work in the endeavor to improve the lot of the poor, the Christian and the Communist may seem to differ more in method than in aims. In St. Luke, the mother of Christ salutes his coming into the world with these words: "He hath showed might in his arm; he hath scattered the proud in the conceit of their heart. He hath put down the mighty from their seat and hath exalted the humble. He hath filled the hungry with good things; and the rich he hath sent empty away." We are told, too, in the *Acts* of the first Christian community that "neither did anyone say that aught of the things which he possessed was his own; but all things were common to them. . . . And distribution was made to every one according to his needs." Engels acknowledged a likeness: "The history of early Christianity has many characteristic points of contact with the present labor movement. . . . Both Christianity and proletarian socialism preach the coming deliverance from slavery and poverty. . . ." Nevertheless, Marx held that "the criticism of religion is the beginning of all criticism." Christianity did do a service when it was founded, but since then it has changed with the changes in society and is now an ally of the capitalists. But even had it kept its pristine purity it would still remain the enemy of communism; and the reason is that it challenges the very basis of Marxism, its materialism. As Engels again said: it is an ideology and the one that is "most remote from its material basis and apparently the most foreign to it." It follows that in contrast with all else which opposes the Marxist analysis religion has nothing whatsoever to offer, and must be treated as inherently false. It is the duty of communism to make war on religion, and, in Lenin's words: "we must not confine the war against religion to abstract and ideological preaching. . . . We must also transfer the combat into all the concrete activities of the class movement, with a view to severing the social roots of religion." The capitalist perversions of science and art can be corrected, but religion spells servitude to a God or to priests and can have no place in a liberated society.

Marx accepted the attitude of Feuerbach to religion and shared uncritically the anti-religious views current in his younger days. Communism has inherited his views and left them unchanged even though it could have found other more fashionable arguments later when the study of comparative religion was in its heyday. The anti-God department of the Communist building is suffering from dry rot. Religion certainly did not begin or continue just as a compensation for miserable conditions or slavery. Such an hypothesis was glaringly against the facts in Marx's day, and the vastly increased knowledge we now have of the history of religion, of the great religions of the past and of primitive religion, has multiplied those facts. Even the psychologists have taken a hand in disposing of the old materialistic theory, and Jung claims to have found from his clinical experience that the divine archetype is the foundational experience of man.

Religion was not born out of poverty and oppression; it is the creative and conserving center of the early communities and tribes, whether pastoral or nomadic. In the theory of Paul Tillich, God is encountered whenever men feel "ultimate concern"; in Rudolf Otto's view, man is religious because he has a sense of the numinous. But it is simpler to regard religion as man's reaction in the presence of nature and of his own human condition, and the expression of this emotional apprehension in worship of their Author. As culture develops, religion is purified. The indirect apprehension of the divine is freed from its confusion with natural effects, reason makes an ascent from the finite to the infinite. In the east the religious geniuses sought for a way out from the illusory world in which the individual lived, convinced as they were that human life is so incomplete as to be unreal. The imperfection of human thought is also Plato's central theme, and no one can accuse Plato of creating religious fancies to compensate for a life of servitude or poverty. The impulse in the great religious leaders always springs from their desire of spiritual perfection. They have been convinced that this world is but a shadow and image of a perfect life, and that human love is but an intimation of a union which must be unchanging and complete. Marx, therefore, is far from understanding or doing justice to the experience which informs all the high religions and sends the mind soaring up beyond time and space.*

Christianity as a religion answers to the general description just given, but it has characteristics which belong to it alone. It claims to be unique and to be the one complete revelation of the will of God. This is not the place to discuss this. What must be said, however, is that even were it granted that Marx has rightly diag-

---

* Marx made a lasting contribution to social history by showing the influence economic conditions have on culture, art, and philosophy. Religion, too, was affected, especially in its myths. The gods of the hunter and shepherd of the city and empire are recognizable from their local accent. But even in the manners and habits of primitive societies there are variations which cannot be accounted for by economics. Mr. David Rigsman, the author of *The Lonely Crowd* and *Individualism Reconsidered,* quotes three primitive societies: one, the Pueblo Indians, who are peaceable and co-operative; two, the Dolu Islanders in the Pacific, who are jealous of women and property and spend their lives trying to get something for nothing by magic, theft or fraud; three, the Kwakiutl Indians of the Pacific North-West who are competitive and so apt to show off that they burn their blankets and their houses. These variations have other causes than economics. Still more true is this of those Eastern exalted, mystical and metaphysical religions, which sprang up in conditions of a primitive economy and a chaotic society. Some of the myths and pantheons can be explained as a reflection on the forms of society to which they belong, but such explanations fail altogether to account for the monotheism of Israel and the words and exhortations of the Living God, who gives the Commandments.

nosed the basis of religion in general, it would not follow that the Christian religion would have to be dismissed with the rest. The reason for this is that Christianity is a historical religion, one based on fact and not on subjective experience or theory. There are writings, whose authenticity and truthfulness can be tested, which record the life of one who is as much a historical figure as Marx himself. These writings are by eye witnesses or by men who were contemporary. The life of the Christ which they tell, his sayings and message, his deeds and character make up the essence of the Christian religion. Who he was, what he did and what he had to say form the Creed, which in shorter or larger form was recited in the first centuries and was regarded as an unchanging summary of the faith. There were many mythical religions which at a first glance resembled the Christian one in that the God dies and comes to life again, and for a time Mithraism competed in popularity with the Christian faith. The differences, however, were decisive even in the very texture of the story; but above all what separated them is the historical reality of Christ, the vivid, actual impression he made upon his disciples. The boast and glory of the Jewish religion lay in its worship of Jahve, the one true God who dwelt on high, whose shekinah or presence made the ark and the temple sacred. The Jews spurned the polytheism of the nations around them and were monotheists *à outrance*. Nevertheless, the disciples of Christ, Jews themselves, did not hesitate to call the man they had known God. "In the beginning was the Word, . . . and the Word was God, . . . and the Word was made flesh and came to dwell amongst us";

and the writer goes on to say that he himself and others had actually seen his glory or shekinah. Another disciple years after Christ had come and gone recalls in a letter that he had been with him on a mountain and seen him, had been an eyewitness of "his exaltation" and heard a voice "out of the splendor which dazzles human eyes" saying: "This is my beloved Son; to him then listen," and that "word," he adds a little later, "will go on shining, like a lamp in some darkened room, until the dawn breaks, and the day star rises in your hearts."

This insistence on the impression made by Christ is not irrelevant. In fact the Christian religion is unintelligible unless it be put in the forefront. The Christian teaching all depends upon it, and in the creed after the first articles on God the creator of all things, we are brought up against this historical as well as theological article, of the Word made flesh who was born in time of a woman, whose name is known. He suffers under a Pilate who has a place in the annals of Rome. Were it not that Christianity believes that God became man and that its faith is a historical one, there would be hardly any point of comparison between the ideal of Marxism and that of Christianity. The great Eastern religions are not interested in history; the works of man belong to the world of illusion. By prayer and concentration of mind the real world will reveal itself. This distinction between the world of appearances or phenomena and the real world is, in fact, so widespread and so agelong that it cannot be neglected in any truthful account of human experience. It is not confined to the East. The Dionysiac religions are inspired by it; on an Orphic tablet is inscribed, "I have escaped from the wheel of life"; Gnosticism, which is ever reviving in some form or other, regards the soul as degraded by its material habitation, and Christianity itself teaches us that we have here no abiding city.

It is a pity that the depth and extent of this religious experience of the insufficiency of temporal life was never grasped by Marx. Christianity shares that experience, but not to the undervaluing of man's temporal state. Now such an experience cannot be ignored or treated lightly in any comprehensive philosophy of man. While this is so, Christianity, nevertheless, claims that it can meet Marx on his own terms and offer a better program for civil life. It has associated itself with human life and one of its aims is to redress society. Many observers have remarked that in contrast to idealistic philosophies and mystical religions Christianity and Marxism come together on a number of points. The first is the connection of both with the Hebrew religion. Marxists would deny that they owe anything to the Bible, but, none the less, it is not easy for a Jew to be entirely uninfluenced by his past. Israel was the "chosen race"; from it the Messiah was to come to restore the kingdom of Israel and bring glory and happiness to his people. The Jewish prophets foretold this great day when "nation shall not lift up sword against nation, neither shall they learn war any more. But they shall sit every man under his vine and under his fig tree, and there shall be none to make them afraid." The images which these prophets used are of material happiness, and the Jews had interpreted these images of an actual, temporal kingdom which was to come. In this regard the Jews and Marx were in agreement. When Christ began to preach, the crowds that listened to him hoped that his good news concerned this coming liberation of the Jews from the Roman domination and the advent of a new supremacy for the Jews. The question to be asked is how far Christ repudiated the idea of a material kingdom to replace it by one which has nothing to do with this world or its values or history. This is a crucial question and must be answered.

Now that every class of person in the world has, to use a Marxist expression, thrown off its chains, the main and almost controlling interest is in the development of national and international societies and their welfare. The ancient simple views of history have been succeeded by an intense study of every period and a strong desire to see the meaning and pattern of it. Societies rise and fall and hand on something to their successors, but what it is they hand on and how far the accumulated wisdom is a possession or a loan, and what we can learn from the past to profit us in the future, these are all matters which are still enigmatic. With the startling increase of power in science and techniques within recent years, it is felt that long acquired habits of civilization can be perverted and the monuments of beauty and knowledge can in a few moments be turned into dust. With the danger of losing at a stroke what we had taken for granted as rocklike in its foundation or as permanently alive and growing, civil life and the creation of civilization become dearer to us, and the values, for which human effort and genius are responsible, and human welfare tend to preoccupy the present generation. For these reasons we find, as we might expect, that some of the defenders of Christianity emphasize its relevance to temporal affairs, to the social and political troubles, and refer the promises of the Gospel to the peace which it is the duty of all members of society to promote. The "other world" is kept in the background or played down, or even, as we have seen in the case of distinguished theologians already quoted, this "other world" is identified with human history and progress. In this sort of exegesis of Scripture the expression "The Son of Man" which Christ uses is made to refer to the proletariat who end our existing class struggles and inaugurate the classless society. Berdyaev, although he criticizes communism for its excessive materialism, plays with a similar idea.

Other Christian writers appear to be burdened with a guilty conscience and feel that Communists have stolen their thunder while they have been apathetic or basking in the sunlight of the rich; or they admit that Christianity has been so uninterested in social injustice, so salvationist in its preaching about the next world, that it deserves the gibe about being the opium of the people. As one says: "The Manifesto and the Internationale were needed in God's providence to bring back to men a hope which was at once genuinely social and inescapably historical." The world was treated as a place where sin was bound to prevail, as a place to be feared by the holy, and due in its time to return to dust and ashes. Such a contrast between the religious and Christian life and the secular one, it is held, is false and has no warrant in the New Testament. Neither the Gospel writers nor St. Paul make such a division. The separation came in later and was due to the infiltration into Christian teaching of the Greek ideas of spirit and matter. The supposedly Christian philosophy which grew up standardized the idea of another spiritual world, which had no contact with our phenomenal world, and this spiritual world was identified with the Kingdom of Christ, the life of grace and the Church. The new highly developed sense of the importance of history, the immense impact made by the Marxist dialectic and its culmination in the good estate of the people, and lastly the rediscovery of the central place eschatology has in the gospel message, have opened the eyes of Christian thinkers to the intimate connection between Christ's teaching on the Kingdom, his incarnation and second coming and the progress of human history. This has brought about a revision of the old distinction between secular history and the spiritual or supernatural life.

How far can this revision be accepted? It ought not to be too difficult to settle this question as we have so much evidence upon which to rely. The Founder of the Christian religion lived and died at a time when the Roman civilization had made communication easy. His disciples were commissioned "to go and teach all nations" his message of good news. This message was sacred and to be kept unadulterated. "For we are not as many, adulterating the word of God, but with sincerity: but as from God, before God in Christ we speak." And "though we, or an angel from heaven, preach a gospel to you, besides that which you have received, let him be anathema." The early Christians, therefore, were taught a set of truths which were recited in their meetings. What these were we know in part from mention of them by St. Paul and by the evidence of Christian writers without a break from the end of the first century. They are defended against the pagan by a series of writers in the second century called the Apologists and from then onward there is the massive witness of celebrated saints and writers in the East and West. We have still some of the early Creeds and the discussions and declarations of the Faith in the famous Councils of the Church.

There were disagreements, indeed, early ones, which served to clarify the message of the gospel. But amongst the truths disputed there is little or no trace of the view that the Christian Kingdom of God and the earthly Kingdom are intended to be one. The emphasis, on the contrary, in the early Church is on the spiritual Kingdom, which is not of this world. The Christians set so much store by their doctrine of immortality that they could hardly believe that the pagan Platonists already believed in an after life. Without a break the doctrine of the two cities or Kingdoms developed, and as the Christian teaching was held to be truth as revealed by God himself, it is not likely that a serious mistake could have crept in without protest. Christianity, as we know, suffered divisions, but not on this point. The Eastern Orthodox Church separated from Rome in the ninth and eleventh centuries, and the disputes turned on points such as the primacy and what is called the *Filioque* clause. The Protestant Churches again broke with Rome on questions of the sole authority of the Bible, the meaning of faith and other such points. They all accepted the tradition of the two Kingdoms because they were agreed at least on certain essential doctrines of Christianity. These were that Christ was God and also truly Man; that He reconciled to God a world alienated by sin by His death on a Cross and Resurrection; that by faith in Him and by His grace men can be brought to salvation, and this salvation, known now by faith, will be realized in immortal happiness in the Kingdom of God.

Such being the content of the Gospel, the distinction of an earthly society and a heavenly society follows inevitably. In the Catholic view, however, the Church is a visible Society and, as embedded in history, it is not entirely "otherworldly" in the sense that Marxists give to the word. Christ had a human nature, and Christians belong to Christ as members of a body belong to it. All that is human, therefore, can be sanctified, and must be reverenced.* As, moreover, the beginning of the Kingdom of God is lived by faith and not by experience in this temporal life, the perfection of the individual, of the family, of the state and of society is of paramount importance. In the official record of Christianity there is, therefore, little or nothing to be found in favor of this suggested revision. But we can learn more perhaps by looking with closer attention at

* The communication of the Christian revelation can be made only through human means—by language, images and thought. Were the Christian faith quite unworldly, it would have to ignore the value of natural truths and natural virtues. The Church has without timidity used human and commonsense certainties as a basis for the supernatural. The natural distinctions of right and wrong, of soul and body, freewill and necessity make intelligible the Christian doctrines of sin and grace and Christ's personality and natures and the possibility of a higher life. For the same reasons Christianity welcomes the advances in scientific knowledge, social progress, and the love of natural and artistic beauty.

one special characteristic of Christianity, its combination of the supernatural and the historical. Recent and careful study of what is called the eschatological element in the New Testament has served to point the contrast between Christianity and, for example, Platonism and many of the great religions of the East.

The felt and reasoned distinction between spirit and matter, which these latter religions taught, is transformed in the Christian faith. God, who is spirit, becomes man, the Word is made flesh, and through his humanity he redeems man and sets the world on a new axis. The God-man is a new Adam who begets a new human race. The body shares the glories which, in pagan thought, had been confined to the spirit, and nature, which on account of its flux and evanescence, was regarded as "half-unreal," is given a new unity and purpose. As God has entered history and has accomplished a divine intention, history cannot possibly be unaffected by such an event. The act of God, which is in our human calendars begun and finished within a small, definite number of years, has a transcendent power and quality which, so to speak, makes it at home in any period of history. It invades history and the transforming power is operative until the end of time and everywhere, as well as in the specially chosen ways instituted by Christ. All that happens, A.D., is signed with his name, whether it be for him or against him. God's timeless act of redemptive love makes every human choice a crisis, for when the Paraclete is come, "he will convince the world of sin and of justice and of judgement." Time becomes a string of "nows" in which the individual and the peoples meet their new fate, which is the acceptance or denial of absolute love. The divine order, which is epitomized in a person, keeps step with the temporal order, and makes the advent of the Word made flesh ever present and up to date. The word in the New Testament which conveys this mysterious truth is the Greek word, *kairos,* the propitious moment and opportunity in the new, historical relationship set up between God and man. It is also a "crisis" and an agony or *agôn,* and in the apocalyptic language of the Gospels, as of the prophets, it reflects one everlasting act or event in the dénouements of time, especially Christ's trysting place with the soul in the chief crises of life, mostly unexpected, such as the crisis of conversion, the cross of affliction and death. So dazzled were the early Christians with the overpowering truth and mystery of this "coming," that, as might be expected, they were tempted to simplify it and translate it into an expectation of a rapid end of the world. Whereas we now see time going on and on with no ascertainable end, many early Christians saw it within their own lifetime as the end of the world. The paradox of Christianity, however, is that time and history are indeed included within the Christian dispensation, though the end is in the beginning and any age or time is the "year of the Lord" and the *kairos* of God.

There can be no doubt, therefore, that in the Christian view the kingdom of God and history are not dissociated, even if we have to admit a contrast between what St. Augustine, in a well-known passage, called the City of Man and the City of God. Within recent years, as explained above, certain Christian apologists have felt the need of bringing Christianity down to earth, and this rediscovered eschatological, as it is called, element in the New Testament has provided them with the means to do so. They now claim that the teaching of Christ in the Gospels, in parables and sermons, has always a reference to life as it is lived here and now on earth, that the religious ideal and human affairs are not kept apart as later they were in a "crude supernaturalism." In this crude later teaching the emphasis turned from this world and the bettering of it to a hope for immortality and the future happiness beyond the grave. This world became a valley of tears, a place given over to evil from which it was the duty of the Christian to retire. The idea of heaven came to be substituted for that of earth; it was the "dear country for which the eyes kept vigil." But in the New Testament there is little trace of such a heaven as this. It is not the haven of the reward, for Christ is he "whom the heavens must receive until the times of the restoration of all things;" just as in other passages we read that Christ is to come back from heaven, that his people are to be resurrected body and spirit, that all things are to be restored, that there is to be a new heaven and a new earth, when "the holy city comes down from heaven like a bride adorned for her husband."

There are, it must be granted, versions of Christianity which deserve to be called crudely supernatural or escapist. No natural virtues are allowed; original sin has so corrupted man that all his works are evil. But such, as we have seen, is not the main tradition of Christian teaching. In their efforts to put right what they think has been neglected, these defenders of an earthly

Christian society have both exaggerated the purely human and social side of the Gospel message and fought shy of the "folly of the Cross." Without this latter Christianity ceases to be itself, and its message is amputated. Human welfare and human goodness have been adopted by God who became man, but at the same time they must be seen in their proper proportions within the purposes of the Redemption. Religion is first and foremost the worship of God or what serves for God in man's thought. God has to be worshiped "in spirit and in truth," and the first truth in Christ's teaching was that God is our Father; that is to say, God is personal and his attitude towards human beings is a loving providence, as that of a Father to his children. The second and completely new truth is that God so loves man that Christ himself, the Word of God and Son, has become man and "dwelt amongst us," in order that he might end the estrangement and bring an atonement of man with God. Christ is to be "the way and the truth and the life," and the new union or Atonement is to be in a form beyond man's dream or conceiving. As Christ is one in divine love with the Father, so those who receive him are to be so united with him that they will form one society or organism and so share in the divine life itself. This elevation of man into a new life, where there is a divine current of love, and a closeness of union symbolized on another level by human marriage, is beyond the natural powers of man, and for that reason has been called supernatural. That is the technical meaning of "supernatural," and all the other meanings which have been attached to it, the extraordinary, the magical, the mystical or unexplainable have little or nothing to do with the precise theological significance of the term. This supernatural life, then, is the keynote of the Christian religion; it is the pearl beyond price of the gospel, the treasure for which everything else must be sold; it is the invitation to the banquet for which all else must be left; and it is that supreme offer of love which is incompatible with compromises, delays, or the allegiance to any other rival love.

So stated, and without further elaborations, this doctrine changes altogether the perspective in which the welfare of human society must be regarded. But there is another historical truth which also affects the whole issue of the relations of the Christian religion to human society, and that is the Cross. The offer of God-made-man was rejected: "He came unto his own and his own received him not;" or as the Creed puts it: "He was crucified, died and was buried; the third day he rose again from the dead." The symbol of Christianity is the Cross, and the Cross lies over the world and marks human history. The rejection by man of God makes a cleavage between the natural and the supernatural, the secular state and the Church. It is quite conceivable that, if Christ had been accepted instead of rejected, the history of the world might have been so different that a perfect society on earth would have flowered into being. This is mere speculation, but the Bible prophecies suggest some such future, and the long and severe training of Israel to prepare it for the advent of the Messiah increases in significance if this be so. Something immense hung upon the choice, and Christ himself regarded his mission to the chosen people as all important, and lamented their blindness: "Jerusalem, which I would have gathered as the hen gathers its chicks under its wing, but thou hast not known the time of thy visitation." Those who see in Christ's words and parables the proof that the kingdom of God would be made manifest in history are relying on a condition, which was within the free choice of man and really possible, but was never fulfilled. The other side of the picture, the prophecy in Isaiah of the Suffering Servant of Jahoe, was turned upmost, and it is in the light of the rejection that we have to understand the sad words of Christ in the discourse on the evening before his death. He speaks to those disciples who have accepted him and been faithful to him, and he separates them from the world which has not known him. "I have manifested thy (the Father's) name to the men whom thou hast given to me out of the world . . . I have given them the word, and the world hath hated them; because they are not of the world, as I also am not of the world. . . . And for them do I sanctify myself, that they also may be sanctified in truth. And not for them only do I pray, but for them also who through their word shall believe in me." They are to suffer and to be persecuted, but from this passage, as from others, they are called to be the witnesses of his truth, to form that divine society on earth which is to spread his word, and be the new form which Christ in his risen life will take to continue as God and man upon the earth and in heaven.

Whatever then may have been the possibilities of a concord between the new Christian society and the earthly society, a covenant of peace and fruitfulness, they were ended at the Crucifixion. Neither the Resurrection nor Pentecost cancel the ominous decision of the world's representatives to bury Christ out of sight in a tomb. From hence-forward the Christian life is to be one of faith in the unseen Christ and not of sight, and to be in the world but not of it. While, for instance, there are in St. Paul's letters passages which refer to the restoration of all things in Christ—some of which have been already quoted—what is dearest to his heart and mind is that he knows "the virtue of his (Christ's) resurrection, and what it means to share his sufferings, moulded into the pattern of his death, in the hope of achieving resurrection from the dead." After his failure at the Areopagus he is more sure than ever what is the new wisdom of God, and so "what we preach is Christ crucified, to the Jews a stumbling block and to the Gentiles folly." No less emphatic is St. Peter: "Blessed be that God, the Father of our Lord Jesus Christ, who in his great mercy had begotten us anew, making hope live in us through the resurrection of Jesus Christ from the dead. We are to share an inheritance that is incorruptible, inviolable, unfading. It is stored up for you in heaven." Finally in the letter to the Hebrews we hear the authentic voice of the early Christian church: "Let us, too, go out to him (Christ) away from the camp, bearing the ignominy he bore; we have an everlasting city, but not here; our goal is the city that is one day to be."

In the light of these texts, chosen at random among so many others, it is impossible to accept the view mentioned above that the ideal of a personal immortality and of "a crude supernaturalism" was a later Greek importation into the Christian faith. Excessive individualism in piety and outlook there may have been; Christians, for instance, living in the nineteenth-century world of individualism run riot, were likely to be affected by its climate. To desire to redress the balance makes for valuable criticism, because Christians belong to a society which is communal in a way communism has not attempted to be. But the note of "personal immortality" is always present, in St. Paul's desire to be freed from the burden of this world, in the old man St. John waiting longingly to see Christ again, and in the famous letter of the martyr, St. Ignatius of Antioch, who died in Rome about A.D. 100. He begs his fellow Christians not to try to save his life. "The pangs of a new birth are upon me. . . . Alive as I am at this moment of writing, my longing is for death. Desire with me has been nailed to the cross and no flame of material longing is left. Only the living water speaks within me, saying: hasten to the Father. I have no taste for the food that perishes nor for the pleasures of this life. I want the Bread of God, which is the Flesh of Christ, who was of the seed of David."

I quote this passage because there speaks in it over eighteen hundred years ago the very spirit of Christianity. What St. Ignatius says is exactly what could be said now of the beliefs of the Church *—the "living water" is baptism and faith, and "the Bread of God"

* The identity in thought, irrespective of time, between Catholic belief in the first and twentieth century is out of step with the process of thought according to the Marxist dialectic. Not the dialectic of opposites but the contemplation of an unchanging and inexhaustible truth is the resource of the Christian philosopher. As, however, the Marxist treats the writings of Marx as inviolate, outliving time and nature's dialectic, he borrows, in defiance of his own principles, from a perennial philosophy.

is the Eucharist and the Christ is the Christ of history, no myth but "of the seed of David." The faith, too, has that ardor which Christianity should have still within it to meet the burning faith of communism, but it does not meet violence with violence. Love and sacrifice are its weapons. The Christians are persons met together in one community or body, with the common virtues of faith, hope, and charity or love. Each of these virtues has a special sense, dependent upon the Christian's relation to Christ. Though no longer visible on earth Christ fulfills his promise to be with his followers "all days even unto the end of the world" by living in a society of his own creation, of which he is the head. The image of a body, of which Christians are the members and Christ the Head or animating principle, is used to express the reality of his presence and the closeness of the love which unites Christ to those who have faith in him. "I no longer live, but Christ lives in me," says St. Paul, and in the Fourth Gospel Christ calls himself the vine: "I am the vine; you the branches; he that abides in me and I in him, the same bears much fruit." The Christian, therefore, while remaining an individual person is caught up into the life of God and made a member of the mystical body of Christ with many others. This is the social body which challenges the claim of the classless society to be mankind's ideal. It does not make any easy promises of a good time to come in this world; it lives in faith and in sure hope of an everlasting happiness and sees in history the slow and even intermittent conquest of evil by love. This society, then, or institution is a kind of ladder between heaven and earth; it worships God and bears witness to God's love for man and teaches the way to friendship with God. This institution is what is known as the Church.

As then this spiritual society has for its end the supernatural union of man with God—man being elevated to a quasi-equality with God in Christ—the supernatural order and the temporal order cannot be identified. Man cannot serve both God and Mammon, but he has duties to both God and Caesar. This looks clear, but the demarcation of the two Kingdoms has proved a difficult and thorny subject of dispute. In the beginning of Christianity, St. Paul and others were content to tell their converts to obey their temporal rulers in all matters which were not sinful. Their minds and hearts were so filled with the "good news" of Christ that they gave a minimum of attention to secular problems. For a long period under the Roman Empire the Christian body was ignored or proscribed and therefore no occasion arose for considering the part Christianity ought to play in society. Changing circumstances here as in other matters brought into play the hitherto undivulged resources of the faith. The Empire waned, and the Emperors moved away from Rome to Ravenna and Constantinople. In their absence and as the Empire gradually collapsed the duty of keeping order fell more and more on the Popes. In the end the Popes became temporal as well as spiritual rulers in Rome; whereas in the Eastern Empire the Church became more and more associated with Imperial rule. Historical circumstances in this way were responsible for different relationships between Church and State. In both East and West a Christian society was formed,

Kings and Bishops, in the West, laymen and clerics living together under ecclesiastical and civil laws. Savage quarrels broke out, but they were over matters of jurisdiction or temporal authority. Both accepted the theory of the two Kingdoms and the State gave priority to the spiritual authority. This at times uneasy union of Church and State in one Christian society came to an end at the Reformation. National churches sprang up and Catholic and Protestant rulers had to face the problem of divided and dissident views amongst their subjects. The State grew in power and in some countries, such as the United States, took up a neutral attitude to the various religions. In other countries there arose a marked hostility to the Christian Church on the ground that it claimed rights and taught beliefs which interfered with the more or less totalitarian tendencies of the governments.

From this historical record it is clear that the Christian Church has had to adapt this doctrine of the two powers or Kingdoms to varying circumstances. But it has done more than adapt itself, for it has come in time to understand and develop the wisdom which is its birthright. As we have seen, in the first centuries there was no call upon the Church to take its part in civil affairs. Only the need of the young barbarian races who had taken over the Empire brought the Church from the cloister to the market place, and in the dark ages the youth and ignorance of the peoples almost dictated the part which Christianity played. This is the period when strong measures were needed to curb barbarian adolescent passions and to lay down the laws and principles of a civilization. The Church had little experience on which to draw, and necessity became the mother of invention. It accepted what it could of the prevailing customs of the races, the "hierarchical" society, with its basis on servitude, and tried to elevate and sanctify each status, royal, knightly, and lowly, on the principle of the nobility of service of God and man. If the Pope was at the apex of this hierarchy it meant that he was the most responsible "servant of the servants of God." The old Christian maxim, "to serve God is to reign" (*cui servire regnare est*) was brought into play, and by this and similar principles a society came into being of which religion was the soul or informing power. The Church acted pragmatically and not with a preconceived idea of what an ideal human society should be like. It realized that the Christian religion required a good soil on which to grow—that the spirit was more free in a healthy body, and therefore human nature must be at its best if the supernatural end of man were to be attained. It sensed, too, that human nature could benefit and be at its happiest where grace abounded. Hence it sought for peace and concord among the nations, for justice and freedom in each Kingdom, and instituted innumerable works of charity; but it was not fully aware that it was creating a society in which the activities of man could multiply, and science, philosophy and art have their own autonomous and valuable ends within the all-embracing end, the love of God.

The lesson which the Church learnt from the great experiment of the Middle Ages was that however otherworldly its aim might be, it could not turn its back on human society. By its very covenant it was committed

to the perfection of the men and women who had to
live their lives in the midst of secular occupations.
Partly, too, by its own action and effort it had created
human societies, which had their own laws of growth
and their own problems, social, political, and economic.
Whereas St. Augustine, in the fifth century, had written
of two cities, the city of Man and the city of God,
whose principles seemed utterly at variance, the
Church, after the fall of the Roman Empire, left alone
in a barbaric world, had to civilize that world and
realized in action that nature could be perfected by
grace and that the good of human society fell within
its care. The Son of God was also the Son of Man. The
full realization of this truth, however, took time and
was delayed by the break-up of Christendom in the
sixteenth century. National Churches were diverted
from the larger issue of society to the problem of religious and political conformity within the State. Certain sects, reverting to the Old Testament, sought to
impose their ideals by the sword. The Catholic Church
looked with misgiving at the results of its commingling
with human concerns. If it had Christianized the dark
ages it had also become tainted with worldliness, even
in high places. For this reason the emphasis once more
turned to unworldliness after the manner of the early
Church. Nevertheless having grown in understanding
of its duties to society, it gave more thought than before to the problems of human rights, the foundations
and purposes of States and the ideals of society.

The data for a more mature philosophy of society
have accumulated in the last three hundred years. The
world of St. Thomas Aquinas was relatively a small

one. Nothing was known of America, little of Africa, and what was known of Asia came from travelers' tales. It was assumed that man's origin dated back only some four thousand years before Christ. The medieval thinkers had a static conception of history and were not, therefore, greatly interested in the evolution of society. They thought, as a result, in terms of the situation which confronted them. Their answers were pragmatic, and it was only the inherent wisdom of the Christian ideal which gave to these answers a lifegiving quality. This quality was such that it enhanced the idea of law, of freedom, and of personality, and led to the true humanitarianism, which is embodied in modern, democratic constitutions. Modern democracy is partly the heir of the medieval conceptions of the common law and the philosophy of man. I say, partly, because many other influences have been at work in the making of modern society. Trade and science transformed life within the states. Nations became more and more independent and isolated their aims from those of the Christian religion. In the Middle Ages the Church stood on the hilltop, and the layman laboring on the slopes looked to it as his protector and destination. As time passed the state assumed more and more control and expected the Church to be its ally and servant. The decisive moment came towards the end of the eighteenth century, and the first seismic portent was the French Revolution. The thought, long brewing, exploded; it was that man was master of his own fate and could, by taking thought and action, create an earthly paradise.

"Liberty, fraternity, and equality" were the terms in

which society, now come of age, first expressed its ideals. The achievement of them looked simple to the people to whom they were first preached, but the history of the last one hundred and fifty years is marked by many setbacks and unexpected pitfalls. One idea which has come to the support of these ideals is that of development or evolution. I have said that in the Middle Ages the conception of development in history was wanting. Now the guiding formula is that of "becoming," of progress in time. As a result numbers of writers have devoted themselves to working out a pattern in history, and part of this pattern, if not the whole of it, is concerned with the possibility of a universal society, which will be by human standards free from want and fear and oppression and vice. The extreme example of such a theory and belief is communism. Christianity in the first centuries brought the gospel to the nations, but perforce had little or no part to play in the affairs of this world. But once it had been drawn into human affairs it produced a temporal society with its own laws and separate end—the Western civilization which in time became strongly independent nations. Some eminent Protestant thinkers, convinced that original sin must bring to nothing all human efforts, see no point in co-operation with them. Other Anglican writers, as we have seen, insist that on a right interpretation of the New Testament there is a more intimate connection between the heavenly city and the earthly city than has been supposed.

The Catholic Church has reacted by taking note of the precise problems of the modern state and providing a practical answer based on principles. These answers can be found in a series of Encyclicals issued from Rome on the nature of the State, its relation to religion, the proper relations between labor and capital, the rights of the laborer, the liberties which must be given free exercise, and the means of insuring international peace. There are Christian groups who mourn for a past age, idealizing medieval society and tracing all modern evils to the failure to abide by its standards and practices. But those who are more level-headed are aware that the clock cannot be put back, and that there are complicated and specific problems now created by modern technology and modern methods of production and distribution, which never existed before. The new problems, as it has been said, "can be analyzed only in terms of the entire social structure in which a man lives and acts, in terms of man's essential need for personal fulfilment in and through and with certain social groups which keep alive the meaning of his existence, the family, the neighborhood, the parish, the small private property which is his own, the association of his working companions." The modern individual is called free, but he is uprooted and depersonalized by the very nature of modern technology and industrial production. Those who seek for answers along the lines of labor unions or big business or State control or totalitarianism miss the point. They are putting their trust in half measures, because the free individual remains uprooted and a commodity to be fitted to the demands of production and efficiency. No man can live fully, unless he is established in a group to which he feels he belongs, one in which he is understood and appreciated and with which he can share his hopes and ideals. Family, friendly neighborhood, loyal associates, all are needed: but above all a community which confirms his sense of responsibility, takes him out of himself, gives meaning and honor to his actions and makes him give thanks for the gift of life.

"Only too often it happens that economic life and the employment of capital are no longer ruled by human needs in their natural and real importance. On the contrary, what needs are satisfied and to what extent, is decided in the interests of capital and its profits. In consequence, it is not man's labor for the social welfare that attracts and uses capital, but capital which moves labor about like pawns in a game of chess. . . . In the divinely willed order man would be master of things by his labor; he would not be dominated by them." These words addressed by Pope Pius XII to the Italian Agricultural Federation in 1946 illustrate the approach of the Catholic Church to the social problems of to-day. It attacks a definite problem or abuse and suggests remedies; it does not take sides with business or with labor, and it has always the moral ideal in view, the while recognizing that the State should settle its own economic and social problems without interference. What is clear-cut is its condemnation of communism on account of its materialist philosophy and atheism. No human society can attain its true end or keep high principles alive without the help of God and of grace. What is less certain is its attitude to the hope of a lasting condition on earth of universal peace and goodwill. But if it does not predict such a society, it shows the only way by which it can be attained.

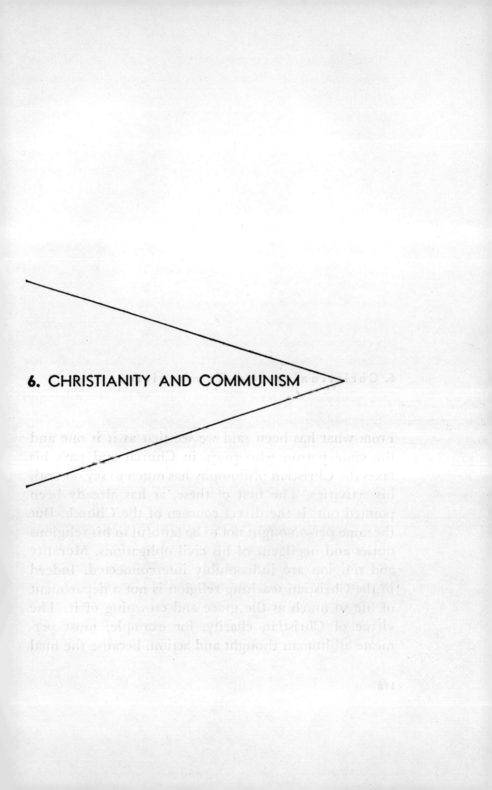

6. CHRISTIANITY AND COMMUNISM

6. Christianity and Communism

From what has been said we see that as it is one and the same person who prays in Church and pays his taxes the Christian philosophy has much to say on both his activities. The first of these, as has already been pointed out, is the direct concern of the Church. But the same person ought not to be faithful in his religious duties and negligent of his civil obligations. Morality and religion are indissolubly interconnected. Indeed in the Christian teaching religion is not a department of life so much as the grace and crowning of it. The virtue of Christian charity, for example, must permeate all human thought and action, because the final end of man governs all he is and does, and as St. Paul says, charity joins us to that end. Furthermore, as it is the same man who is religious, political, and social, a philosophy must insure that he is capable of being all of these. To make any sense of the Christian revelation, man must be allowed to be capable of sin and of repentance, to have a soul as well as a body. From a correct understanding of what man is we can go on to discuss the nature of the individual person, his relations with other men and with a society, what possibilities are open to him of improvement and of establishing a lasting peace upon this earth. The fact, therefore, that Christianity is first and foremost concerned with Christ's "good news of everlasting life," does not mean that it will exclude from its doctrines all that is not strictly revealed and new. The groundwork of man's nature must be firmly established, and more than the groundwork, since the Christian philosophy claims to be all embracing.

The Marxist and the Christian philosophies, therefore, meet headlong on their different conceptions of man, and it is on this issue that debate between the two is easiest. Judgment, however, is often passed on quite other grounds. The history of Communist rule and of its activities since the revolution in Russia of 1917 has roused violent indignation and horror. Such indifference to human life and such brutality were thought to be enough in themselves to condemn the system. "By their fruits you shall know them." But an argument such as this will be countered by the Communist and lends itself to an unending dispute on facts and their evidence. One Communist retort is that Christianity lives in a glass house and cannot throw stones; it has persecuted the Jews, martyred heretics, and encouraged massacres. Although at one period Protestants equally with Catholics imprisoned and tortured their adversaries and led them to the stake and the scaffold, it is the Catholic attitude and its inquisition which are generally quoted. That these persecutions took place in days long past, when intolerance was accepted and harsh methods almost universally approved, weakens the force of the argument but does not remove its sting. Much has been written on this matter and will be written, but the issue is really one of the right to be intolerant. It is impossible to treat such a large subject here at length. Gentleness and respect for other persons are of the essence of Christianity and our present attitude is the fruit of Christian teaching; but in the rough soil of human nature these virtues have taken a long time to develop and be accepted universally. Whatever be said of former persecutions in the West, there is no comparison in scale with those carried out under the Communist régime. Nor can the policy be attributed to the accident of time and period; it belongs, as Whittaker Chambers points out in *Witness,* to the very creed of materialistic communism. Chambers describes the great purge in Russia which lasted from 1935 to 1938 and resulted in the death of vast numbers of men and women variously estimated from several hundred thousand to several millions. "The human horror of the Purge," Chambers says, "was too close for me to grasp clearly its historical meaning. I could not have said then, what I knew shortly afterwards, that, as Communists, Stalin and the Stalinists were absolutely justified in making the Purge. From the Communist standpoint, Stalin could have undertaken no other course, so long as he believed that he was right. The Purge, like the Communist-Nazi pact, later on, was the true measure of Stalin as a revolutionary statesman. That was the horror of the Purge—that acting as a Communist, Stalin had acted rightly."

The word "purge" used for the killing of human beings has that clinical association which the Communist would not deprecate. The story is told of Borodin, I think, that on being rebuked by a Christian nonconformist on the Russian treatment of Christians, he replied that if Christians behaved like St. Paul they would be worth cultivating, but so rotten had they become that they must be cut out like a gangrenous limb if society were to regain its health. In other words, unsentimental surgical operations are necessary for the sake of producing the perfect society. But though the language is biological, the echoes heard in it are ethical and religious. "It is fitting that one man should die for the people." "The final criterion is the safety of the people." Without a faith and without a moral motive no revolutionary cause can inspire devotion and succeed. The vision of the end dominates the Communist to the extent that all is permissible which will serve to its attainment. This is the doctrine that the end justifies any means, and apart from its being, as the Christian philosophy holds it, an intrinsically wrong doctrine, it leads also to tyranny and the police state in the hands of any persons except saints. The Communist, on the other hand, regards it as a higher form of morality, the new form of morality which is superseding the old, bourgeois one. As an official Russian publication on the Capitalist system states it: "From the point of view of Communist ethics only what aids the destruction of the hated features of the bourgeoisie, of the old capitalist world of exploitation and poverty, only that which goes to build the new Soviet, Socialist order is moral and ethical. Soviet patriotism is the most profound manifestation of a new ethic, a Communist ethic, a new psychology of man. Soviet patriotism is the highest stage of moral behavior and ethics in man and society. Purging the mind of man of vestiges of capitalist ethics, the Soviet, Socialist system has formed and developed new ethical values in the human character; loyalty to the leader, to the Soviet homeland, loyalty to one's native party, and loyalty to the Party and the Government." The behavior of Russian Communists has been formed on these new principles, and it explains the passionate loyalty shown to the Party and the readiness of those accused of deviationism to agree with their accusers and accept their punishment.

This ethic, which shocks those brought up on the Greco-Roman civilization and the Christian religion, attracts the modern *déraciné* mind by the clarity of its formula. Uncertainty is exchanged for a clear-cut policy, almost a business-like one, which says: this is what you must do if you really want what you are asking for. Up to now, says the Marxist, morality has been a pretense, the poor were kept with their noses to the grindstone while the rich talked of the virtue of work and serving God. Marx uncovered this hypocrisy and dispelled the shadows round the meaning of morality. The one ideal for man is to be at peace with himself, with nature and society. So far he has been alienated from himself, making false gods, false images of himself and of other men. Now at length he has discovered the pattern of history and the freedom which comes from knowing the necessary laws of life. The people have come to maturity and self-consciousness and can end the struggles which have been going on because of the division of man with himself. A society is coming into being which will be classless and free, one in which men will be able to live a full human life. This is what is good and all else must be judged good or bad by the way it helps or hinders the achievement of that end. Here is a clear standard for judging the morality of any action.

This is the strength of the Communist position. But it is open to the most serious criticism. A student of Marx might well ask how it escapes from being like all the theories which have preceded it, namely, a super-structure which reflects the economic conditions of the time and must therefore change with them? To say that it is privileged is to beg the question, and means in fact that an absolute truth has been surreptitiously introduced into a system which boasts that it is founded on matter which is ever in process of change. Then again we are left uncertain whether the dialectical process still determines the theory or whether the theory is now in charge of the process. This uncertainty marks also the theory of freedom, of which more will be said later. It is one thing to say that freedom is the consciousness of necessity; it is quite another thing to say that man can master necessity and turn it to account. This must mean that the will stands above the stream of necessity, like a signalman directing trains or a yachtsman tacking to make most use of the winds and tides. The uncertainty here manifests itself, also, in the curious change-over in Marx and Lenin from economics to politics. In the structure of Marxian theory economics is the determining factor in the changes of society. When, however, we turn to practice, politics, which in the original briefing belonged to the accidental superstructure, begins to take first place, until now politics seems to have absorbed everything else.

The classless society is the end according to the Communists, and it is this end which gives ethical value to all the means which can bring it about. This is a fundamental dogma, and if asked how does he know it to be true, the Communist must answer that he is philosophically and scientifically certain of it. The processes of nature, as exhibited in the field of economics, are predictable, as predictable as in any other field, say of physics and chemistry. Scientifically, therefore, the classless society can be predicted. So too the only philosophical sense which can be given to terms, such as good and bad, is to take what is fully human, that is existence in the classless society, and to call that and all that serves as means to it good.

The whole argument rests on the accuracy of Marx's materialistic conception of history. It is *a priori* to the degree that it determines what must be man's happiness without inquiring what men actually do desire. For this reason it has to sweep aside a vast amount of evidence that men desire other forms of happiness from that laid down. Then from what must be the theory passes without delay to say it ought to be. The "ought" of morality cannot come from scientific necessity or from the urge to bodily happiness. The classless society may have to come by necessity; it may be what the workers of the world will enjoy, but it does not follow that they are bound morally to do all in their power to produce it. An absolute has crept in or rather strayed in from another world. That men and women feel moral obligation to be an absolute is tacitly admitted in the Marxist theory that in earlier days they invented a God to explain obligations. Not only is the obligation an absolute, but the nature of the end of man is also one, an absolute certainty which it is a crime to question. It rests on the truth of dialectical materialism, and has the same certainty as that. But not only is this truth open to many objections; it is also at first sight incompatible with a final situation in which the dialectic is no longer operative. Moreover the Communist leaders are strangely reticent about the exact nature of this classless society. Its main feature is that there will be no competition but a material distribution from each according to his ability and to each according to his needs. Happiness will follow in such perfect conditions, but Lenin, for instance, was realist enough to put away dreams of everyone behaving perfectly. We are not told how long it is to last, and as there is nothing beyond it, the problem of boredom will arise. Experience shows that human beings must have changing fashions, styles and tastes, and that no matter how just a ruler Aristeides is he will be turned out of office after a time by the bored citizens. The prospect of the classless society going on forever is a grim one, even if the first years are pleasant. But in fact descriptions of it seem drab, for man does not live on bread alone. Nor can the monotony be relieved by adventure or original art and thought. Security has been gained at the expense of risk and novelty, so that many human virtues and qualities will rust unused. Thought, whether philosophic or imaginative, all that is "fancy bred," is a superstructure of changing economic conditions and ideology. The consequence is that in the classless society the ideology must be stationary whatever it is, and it is not clear what the ideology can be. Human beings must suffer when thought and art come to a standstill.

Such a future society may well fail to attract many. All the same they will not be at liberty to look elsewhere. The new morality imposed upon the world by communism says that those who do not like it must be forced to like it or be liquidated. "Replacing objective analysis by 'feelings,' to any extent, threatens catastrophe," and so the "only permissible question about any policy under consideration by the Party is: Will it strengthen the power of the Party?" Koestler, therefore, is not caricaturing the Communist when he makes one of his characters say that the Communist must learn "to strip himself of every scruple in the name of a higher scrupulousness, and to challenge the hatred of mankind because of his love for it. . . ." The Communist morality is based on a special kind of utilitarianism. Utilitarianism has always made an appeal because it provides a very simple measure for deciding what is good and bad, and in many concerns of daily life we do tend to use such a yardstick. If our end is good health then acids and sugar become good or bad according as they help or impair it. But all attempts to build a morality on it have broken down, because we have to settle first of all what is the end of life and then find out what does help towards it; and on neither of these matters is there an easy and obvious solution. Most would say that happiness is what everyone instinctively and deliberately wants, but happiness is of many sorts. Communism says it lies in the classless society; the hedonist, in exquisite pleasures, momentary or permanent; the philanthropist looks to the "greatest good of the greatest number;" the stoic, to virtue for its own sake. The Christian says that it lies in that happiness which comes from the exercise of man's highest faculties lifted up to the knowledge and love of God, who is perfect goodness and truth, and that happines will be found in the perfect community of which the head and animating spirit is Christ.

From no single one of these descriptions of happiness is it easy to deduce what are the good means and what the bad. The fact is that we must already have some elementary distinctions in our mind of what is good and bad before we can formulate or devise standards of conduct. This of itself is enough to disprove the utilitarian theory, and it must be obvious that it is quite arbitrary to say that actions can only be judged by their consequences. Such a statement implies that we already know what is good and what is bad—at least in the "consequences"—and there is no clear reason why we should put off the evil—or rather the good—day until the last. The commonsense, as well as the Christian, view is that certain acts are intrinsically wrong and that it is vicious to do them for a good end. Certain actions in the lives of Julius Caesar, Henry VIII, and Napoleon we condemn; they stain their characters, even as blood stained the hands of Lady Macbeth. We abhor the gas chambers and the extermination of the Jews in the Nazi concentration camps, and no excuse could justify in our eyes such actions. For the same reason the new morality of communism which can permit its members to be liars and double-faced, to make agreements which they have no intention of keeping, to commit wholesale murders and blame the innocent for them, such so-called morality is an impeachment of the whole system making what is foul fair. It is not surprising if ex-Communists and critics wonder whether the end, for which such practices are praised, may not turn out to be sub-human instead of ideally human as the Communists assert it to be. What could happen was depicted in *1984*, that novel which shows society in the thrall of power, conditioned to a sub-human existence by Big Brother and the Ministry of Thought. Such forebodings are based not on any theory but on what is happening in a state where unlimited and centralized power is used without scruple for an end in view. The Communist morality does not allow for the retroactive effect of its teaching on those who put it into practice. The injustice used to win justice usurps the first place, power is used to increase power, and the taste for cruelty becomes ingrained. Those in power forget that the men and women who are to compose the future happy society are of the same stuff as those who are being disciplined, brainwashed, or liquidated to-day to produce that society. These latter are to serve as manure for the future harvest.

The goal of all Communist effort is in the future, and in a future which Lenin realized would not come too quickly. This putting off of perfection to the end is a great drawback in communism. A social theory normally is aware of defects in contemporary society and aims at correcting those defects. Such an aim is necessarily limited. But a philosophy which claims to be all embracing and to say the last word about man ought not to exclude from its good news all those who have ever lived and even those who will have to live before a classless society comes into being. When moreover the living are to have no other purpose than to be sacrificed for the chosen remnant, the picture presented becomes too like that of an ancient slave society, the only difference being that it extends through all time except the last period. The defect is hidden because of the extraordinary habit men have of projecting themselves into a future which they will not live to see. This spirit of self-sacrifice for a cause has been enlisted time and time again, and it is usually to preserve one's country or remedy some evil. This is intelligible if the cause fall within a large philosophy of life which inculcates other reasons and motives for living. The Christian, for instance, has not to regard his life as finished if he surrender it for his friend. But in the Marxist philosophy the individual is totally extinguished or given over to this living servitude. He is nothing more than an instrument to be used and thrown aside; this is his lot and he must fulfill it. What usually keeps him from realizing this is another trick which the mind plays. When a man is in misery or suffering he longs to be free of it, and from his sick bed or prison he forgets the dullness of ordinary life outside and thinks of it in terms of enthusiastic expectation. What is not the painful present has no shadows; it stands for happiness. Similarly he who is attacking present grievances is so emotionally won over to the future that he seldom looks at it soberly and critically. The words "classless society" bring an emotional response and coalesce with his inarticulate ideals, and he forgets he will not be there to enjoy it.

The Christian morality is of a very different kind, and it is to some extent familiar to us in the Western codes of law and established habits of behavior. But though it is known in practice its theory has dropped out of mind or been befuddled by the multiple theories of ethics which have taken their turn to be the fashion in universities. From the Marxist standpoint there cannot be any permanent morality such as that of Christendom. This is true in a way different from that meant by the Marxists. The various philosophies, especially in the last two centuries, have been adopted in part at least by Protestant and nonconformist thinkers, and therefore we find variations in the analysis and interpretation of ethical principles. These philosophies have, however, been written by Christian thinkers, such as Berkeley or Kant, and what is accepted from them has been set in the Gospel context. The traditional ethical system, which is still to be found in the Catholic teaching, has a recognizable character. It is founded on the Aristotelian and Neo-Platonic philosophies and the Ten Commandments, as they provide a basis for the Christian conception of God and man. What the Communist says is that the structure of morality reflects the economic conditions of the time, and that according as they change, so will the moral conceptions and regulations. He argues that the laws during the feudal period were fashioned on the relations of landowner to serf, and, during the predominance of the bourgeois, on the relations of capitalist to laborer. There is enough evidence for such a view to make it plausible. Undoubtedly the emphasis in the Middle Ages is on land and property and transgressions against the right of the owners were punished with a severity altogether out of proportion in our eyes to the offense. So too in the eighteenth and early nineteenth centuries the scales of justice were weighed heavily in favor of the employer. Not till the working class united and was able to fight for living conditions and living wages, were they conceded. Those who make the laws, if they do not take for granted what has been long custom, are always inclined to favor themselves. But while this is so it does not prove that moral ideas are completely dependent on social conditions. The evidence, indeed, supports just the opposite conclusion. What is most remarkable is the clear presence in the varying societies of an ideal of justice and of a set of principles which, though misapplied in practice, are right and permanent in theory. To take a simple example. If we compare the Jewish, Persian, Greek, and Roman ideas about telling the truth, we find that truth telling is a virtue, and the variations do not show that the idea is a purely relative one but that, according to the different conditions and perhaps even characters, the occasions on which saying what is not true is permissible or praiseworthy, vary. So too now in a civilization where persons are much more sensitive than formerly to the feelings of their neighbors, there are many who hold that a dying person should not be told this state. They would be outraged, however, if their view were taken to mean that they thought truth telling was not a virtue.

Writing at a time when the sedulous study of the Middle Ages had not yet begun, Marx assumed that it fitted his dialectic. We know now that the relations between master and serf, lord and vassal were very complicated, and one truth stands out, namely, that economics did not wholly determine the social and economic ideas of the time. The Christian conception of man was a powerful factor. This conception shines out in one of the earliest Christian letters, that of St. Paul to Philemon. A runaway slave had come to St. Paul in Rome, and St. Paul writes to his master, sending him back, but with the message that Philemon is not to think of him "any longer as a slave; he is something more than a slave, a well loved brother, to me in a special way; much more, then, to thee, now that both nature and Christ make him thy own. As thou dost value thy fellowship with me, make him welcome as thou wouldst myself."

It is this ideal running unchanged throughout the changing conditions of Europe, which modified the old slavery laws of the pagan world. It was combined with an idea of social hierarchy where rank was judged on the degree of service to God and man, and also by the theory of contract. A typical instance of the influence of the religious view of man is seen in the statement: "Whoever in the name of the holy and undivided

Trinity, moved by charity, permits anyone of his servile dependents to rise from the yoke of servitude to the love of liberty, may surely trust that in the Last Day he himself will be endued with everlasting and celestial liberty." This comes from the early Middle Ages. Later we find the full expression of the meaning of liberty by the Seneschal of Burgundy. He was speaking at a meeting of the States General of France on the death of Louis XI. He said: "It is certain that the royal power is a dignity and not the property of the prince. History relates that at first the sovereign people created kings by their votes. It is in its own interest that each nation gives itself a master. The whole world repeats that the state is the creation of the people. If it is so, how could the people abandon its charge? How can flatterers attribute supreme power to the prince who exists only in virtue of the people?" To complete this picture of liberty in feudal days one more passage, taken from G. Tellenbach (*Church, State and Christian Society*) will suffice. "There were two kinds of order," he writes, "the eternal order of all creatures round God, the earthly order of men and things. Medieval man knowing original sin tried to make the earthly order correspond with the divine. Hence to have a standing before God and the law was the positive meaning of *libertas,* and implied taking the place assigned to the individual by the first law of creation: 'to each his own.' " During this same period the Common Law, the work of clerics and one of the greatest achievements of Western civilization, came into being. It was fated to become the directive behind the constitutional liberties of the English-speaking world, passing from England to the United States and the then colonies. There was, therefore, no violent break between the modern law and the medieval law. Out of the principles laid down by Bracton and Fortescue have come the rights and liberties of all individuals within the state. Such a steady growth bears out what was said about the permanence of the Christian morality and runs counter to the Marxist theory of morality as a passing superstructure.

As stated in the quotation just given the medieval Christian distinguished between an eternal order and an earthly one, and believed that it was his duty to "make the earthly order correspond with the divine." This statement still expresses a Christian ideal, and it is, so to say, an intellectual donation of Constantine, devised by the early Church after it had come into contact with the pagan wisdom. The Aristotelian and Neoplatonic ideas are borrowed and subordinated to the Christian dogma, that man was made in the likeness of God. This likeness lies specifically in man's possession of an immaterial mind and soul. As partly spirit man can share in the spiritual kingdom and liken himself by knowledge and the love of truth to God himself. The vague but rich Platonic conception of "assimilation to the highest" is, however, transposed onto a new and higher key. Though the early Christians believed that they had a new and unique revelation from God they came to realize that it must be communicated and studied in a language which would be intelligible, and, moreover, that it must be planted where a subsoil would allow the vine to flourish. More than that: in order to understand human nature better, we have to compare it with that of the higher animals and see what is common and where the differences lie; similarly, in order to grasp the new elevation of man into a supernatural union with Christ, we have to take over the highest ideas which natural man can reach and read in and through them the ineffable mysteries of the Christian revelation. This is the plan followed both in the Pauline letters and in the Fourth Gospel, where natural images and ideas are multiplied with the intention of making more clear the new grace given to mankind. With the same purposes the leading writers of the early Church pored over the best philosophical writings until they succeeded in presenting to the world a philosophy which acted as a handmaid to the Word made flesh.

This philosophy, while its first aim was originally to serve the Christian faith, developed in time and through the fierce mêlée of discussion its own relative independence. That is to say, unlike the faith which rests on the word of God, it relies on reason, and stands or falls by its truth. The Christian philosopher, therefore, in disputation with the Marxist does not seek an ally in his faith; he claims that his view of man, for example, is right and that the Marxist fails to give a true picture of human nature by trying to explain it entirely on materialistic lines. As compared with the Platonist the Christian is a realist, but not to the extent of agreeing with Marx. Mr. M. B. Foster says truly that "Hebraic materialism carries with it also a thisworldly concern. If God cared enough for the world to expend his love in fashioning it, it cannot be man's business simply to escape from it!" What is more, if

God became man, then the whole of man, body as well as spirit, must be regarded as exceedingly precious. But Marx will have it that spirit is only a form of highly developed matter, and he tries to stretch his material principles so as to include all thought, the very power, even, to be self-conscious and to judge on the truth of his theory about matter. The Christian philosopher says that this latter feat is impossible and makes nonsense of the theory, for as Professor J. B. S. Haldane, for many years a warm admirer of communism, says: "In order to escape from the necessity of sawing away the branch on which I am sitting, so to speak, I am compelled to believe that mind is not wholly conditioned by matter." The Christian, therefore, does not say of spirit and matter "either or" but both, and his position is that man is composed in one natural union of spirit and matter, soul and body. Man is not a spirit allied to a body, more or less at home in it, nor a body which has higher material functions called spiritual. The individual "I" has its own body and its own mind, and as our actions and thoughts proceed from one ultimate principle, all that can be discovered by chemistry or biology of the interpenetration of the two and of the physical influences of the body on the soul is welcome.

This philosophical conception of man, when enriched by the Christian belief that God created man in his own likeness, that he has an imperishable soul, and that God so loved man as to die for him, has been the leaven which made the new mixture of Western civilization. Rulers and teachers could never quite forget that the individual had become of infinite price.

The purpose of the state was to promote the well-being of the individuals in it, to increase their liberty and so to educate them that they could use their independence and choose for themselves. The value of property turned on this, that each man should own enough to be able to work for himself as well as for the community and so develop his proper personality. Laws ought to be framed so as to protect the common welfare and at the same time protect the innocent and assist them in their proper avocations. No one was to be used as a means; each one had the right to an inner life and the claims of the spirit were higher than those of the body. Even so the body, too, was holy, and to be treated with reverence. The earth was the Lord's and the knowledge and use of it were good. Hence science and art were encouraged, and the old, pagan fear of nature as evil or hostile banished.

These and many other developments came about as the Christian conception of man permeated Western society. It would be ridiculous, of course, to claim that these changes in attitude and treatment came about smoothly or without frequent reverses. A moral ideal has to work through time for its full meaning and for its implications to be realized; and nature is ever recalcitrant. The main capital sins can be seen on every page of history, Christian as well as pagan. The hierarchy of service slides down into class distinctions and pride of place; patriotism passes into aggressive nationalism, the right to own into avarice. A Communist can point to hatreds and bigotries and scandals within the pale of religion itself and cite massacres and burnings and the shocking trade in slaves from Africa to North

America. Such scandals are prophesied in the gospels, and their number has been legion. But the redeeming feature is that in the Christian civilization such scandals were known to be such, and the conscience of Christendom stirred against them to such a degree that in time it lessened those which could be remedied by legislation. China and India compete with Europe in art and philosophy and mysticism, but the customs of exposing infants, of suttee and hara-kiri mark a different attitude to human life from that of the West. The Communists during war are prepared to throw away lives in an assault to an extent which would not be tolerated by countries with a Christian background. Their treatment of prisoners shocks us, as did their extermination of kulaks and the mass deportations in the Baltic States. This contrast between the Christian and Communist attitude to the individual human person is brought out in a leader in *The Times* of August 18, 1954. The writer first quoted from a speech of Mr. Beirut, chairman of the Polish Communist Party, to the effect that the Communist régime had "restored to the working people the highest human dignity and secured the rights due to them." This is the common language of the Western democracies, but the leader writer points out that while various rights, such as the right to work, to free medical care, to insurance, pensions, form part of the new constitution built on the Soviet model, nevertheless these "social services are a weapon in the hands of the State, to be used as incentives, rewards, or punishments as the needs of the State require." The peasant class, for instance, has up to now had little benefit from them. Even the medical services are used for political ends. "The doctrine underlying health services under Communist rule was summed up three years ago by Mr. Zapotocky, Prime Minister of Czechoslovakia. 'Not even the doctors,' he said, 'have a proper appreciation of the needs of production. Widespread are the philanthropic, liberal and incorrect views that the main thing is to help and support the individual.' What kind of a socialist point of view is that? What is required is the protection of production. Damage to a worker's health is not so serious as economic damage in production."

There are some who say that theory does not matter, that, whether we call the soul material as the Communists do or spiritual as do the Christians, the results are much the same. That this is not so the words of Mr. Zapotocky prove. Neither the Marxist nor the Christian makes the mistake of despising dogma and doctrine, and they both keep doctrine and practice near together, though in a different way. The Marxist says that action comes first, but nevertheless it is inseparable from theory. What is wrong is abstract theory divorced from action; this is the Menshevist heresy, that of the armchair philosopher. "The philosophers have only interpreted the world in various ways, the point is to change it." Those who play a game know the rules, those who are in a battle know what is required to win it. Lenin and Stalin had the task of keeping both theory and practice alive without allowing either to be separated, and the violence of their language on this subject shows how much they had it at heart. The Christian has as his model Christ who said of himself that he was "the way and the truth and the life." In these words theory and practice are also joined, but the Christian maintains that no matter how far thought may seem removed from act, if it be true, it must prevail in time. An individual should put an ideal into practice; otherwise he is behaving as less than a full man. There must, moreover, be the opportunity for those qualified to go into their study or their laboratory to devote themselves to pure theory. Pure thought is inestimable both for its own sake and for the good of mankind. In this emphasis Christian differs from Marxist philosophy. The indirect as well as the direct importance of doctrine is seen in the instance of human nature. If human nature is half spirit and half matter and not wholly material, and if through that spirit man is made like to God, much more reverence is due to the individual. The presence of spirit gives him the power to call himself an independent self, self-conscious and to a point self-sufficient, sufficient to the extent, that is, that he must be treated as a person. As partly spirit, this person has also the power, however immaturely and faintly, to grasp truth and to live by standards which are true and absolute; lastly, as created in the likeness of God, the individual has an end which cannot be satisfied except by union with the source of all being, of all love and goodness, God himself. In the light of this conception human nature takes on a new meaning which infiltrates into all departments of society. The Marxist, incidentally, argues that religion is only a drug invented to appease the oppressed and that it has no place in a proper social life. This is a mistaken notion, based on the fact that biological man does not need it as a function. But the same argument could be used against all higher education. Children usually show no disposition at first for learning; they have to be taken to school and forced to learn. The love of learning, which must have been there in human nature, develops after a time and sometimes slowly. The hardworking parents may feel that this schooling is a waste of time; nevertheless, it is the Platos, da Vincis, and Newtons who exemplify the potentialities of human nature.

Plekhanov laughed at the wiseacres who after the French Revolution got as far as saying that politics depended on social conditions and social conditions on property, but when pressed further fell back on reason or "the qualities of human nature." Such explanations, he thought, were amateurish and explained nothing. Marx, on the other hand, does offer a scientific explanation and one that can be tested, when he says that the answer lies in the mutual relations into which men by necessity enter in the social process of production and in the struggle for existence which follows. Let us admit that as against the rationalists and the Hegelians who sought the one key in the movement of thought, Marx did come down to reality and showed one of the factors which affect the development of society. But if Hegel labors one fact too much, Marx falls into the same error. The Christian philosopher is on his side in looking to material causes. He is equally convinced that we cannot neglect the material factor because man is a rational animal and not an immaterial being. The vital question is to what extent material causes determine human life and history, and in the answer to it the aid of science is needed and expected. The scientific attitude is, however, not the same now as in the days of Marx and Engels. It is much more tentative, and while more and more has been discovered about the influence of the body on emotions, temperament, and general outlook, research into the unconscious and into paranormal phenomena has tended to keep the balance as between psychical and physical causes. The present situation is well illustrated in the law courts in the difficulty of deciding whether crimes are committed with a sound or unsound mind. What is assumed in these cases is that a man can act with proper awareness of what he is doing and be able to choose, and, unless the evidence of experts is convincing that this is not so, his freedom of choice is presumed. Behind this presumption is the Christian philosophy of the interaction of two distinct principles, the material and the spiritual, and at the same time the readiness to admit that in human conduct much more must be attributed to the material cause than was once suspected.

The Christian does not deny that a modern man is more likely to approve of and embrace a society of peace and comradeship than the primitive, but the reason for this is not that economics has forced the issue on him; it is rather that he has become more humane, and that in particular the Western culture and religion have nurtured such a desire. What he will not admit is that it was intrinsically impossible for man to have taken another line than that which Marx supposes; or again, for that matter, that it is intrinsically impossible for modern man to reject the Communist solution. There were wise and gentle men before Marx and before Solon. As a generalization it can all the same be admitted that civility and wisdom take time to develop; that primitive man is less in charge of his feelings and passions. But the integration of feelings and passions is achieved by general experience more than by economics, and it is the reason or logos in man, which, by looking before and after and measuring the importance of what happens within and without in the light of some ideal, is most responsible for culture and civilization. Reason of itself does not make a man moral, as it can be used equally by a gang of thieves and a charitable organization, but it does help to clear away the clouds which hang over the ultimate end or purpose of life; a knowledge of the end, as it is hoped, will give meaning to what a man is engaged on doing in the present. As our desires are so vagabond and run so hot and cold, the calm of reason is constantly disturbed by them, and it is this which explains the, at first, disturbing variety in ethical codes. Even where the ultimate end is fixed, social and political conditions may blind the mind to the good and evil in the means. Where women are scarce, or flocks, or gold, such stress may be laid on marriage and the possession of food or the means to obtain it that almost all other issues are subordinated to them. Let a tribe be surrounded by more powerful neighbors: then the birth of male children becomes paramount. The Marxist concentrates on the economic crisis of modern civilization, and in consequence his morality is dictated by it. This comes to saying that the excesses and defeats of moral ideas, which occur like an epidemic in human history, come from this overemphasis on some particular need of an age. Love, for instance, blinds as well as it enlightens. Most of us know how hard it is to see more than one side of a question on which we feel strongly. Hence prejudice, partisanship, and bigotry are so common. Fairness of mind is rarer than supposed, and that can be attained only by standing off from ourselves, our passions and our ideologies.

The Communist does not admit the right to a personal private life or the existence of a world of thought and aspiration which lies beyond social purposes. This does not preclude him, however, from demanding of party-members a self-discipline not unlike that of a religious order. He must disregard money and married life and make himself an obedient instrument of the will of the leaders of the Party. He comes near to practicing the vows of poverty and chastity and obedience, which religious orders take. But his poverty is not of the spirit to find the "kingdom of heaven." Nor does he accept that view of life which encourages the pursuit of truth for its own sake and the life of the spirit as exemplified in the Buddha, Socrates, and Epictetus, to say nothing of the series of Christian contemplatives. It could be argued that St. Benedict and his brethren, who withdrew from the world to live the monastic life, did more than any economists to make possible the writings of Marx; for it was they who above all preserved the learning of the ancient world and so handed on the torch of learning from which Marx, like others, had to light his way. The world would be a sadly impoverished place without the contemplatives and the poets, who can hold infinity in the palm of their hand or see life staining "the white radiance of eternity." Marx himself was fond of Shakespeare and quoted Dante; the present régime in Russia encourages the ballet and other forms of art. But behind the encouragement is the never ceasing purpose of propaganda, the enlistment of the arts in the service of communism. It is hard to see how art and intellectual pursuits, when separated from political action, can be regarded as more than a pastime. It must be an additional reason for the Soviet leaders to discredit the economics of Maynard Keynes when they read his description of the views he and his Bloomsbury friends held: "Not only had social action as an end in itself dropped out of our ideal, but the life of action generally, power, politics, success, wealth, ambition; whilst the economic motive and the economic criterion were less present in our philosophy than with St. Francis of Assisi, who at least made collections for the birds."

By crowding all meaning and all human purposes into a social program and ideal, communism is forced to leave out much that we are accustomed to associate with a contented and happy life We have to feel ashamed for being academic, dilettante, and bourgeois. But it may be objected that Christianity does the same and berates those who spend their lives on mortal joys instead of denying themselves all human pleasures in the quest of everlasting happiness. "Vanity of vanity," said Ecclesiastes: "vanity of vanity, and all is vanity!" Variations on this theme have been so frequent in religious literature and on the lips of preachers, that the Communist does not lack ammunition to turn the position against Christianity. The answer is not simple, though it can be given shortly. The Christian preacher is engaged on correcting the balance between this world's treasures and the next life. The attraction of what can be seen and felt and enjoyed now is naturally more powerful than the promise of what is only dimly realized behind and beyond the shadows of death. Hence, in the parables of the Gospels the emphasis is on the transitory joys of this world and of the danger of setting our heart upon them. The rich man heaps up treasures and suddenly he loses them by death. Those who build on sand instead of on rock are foolish. But the point is not that this life has to be denied as of no worth. On the contrary in this life we have to make the fullest use of the talents which have been given to us. The more we make of life, the greater the reward. The reason for this liberality is that the end, as conceived by a Christian, consists in worshiping and pleasing God, and such an end not only allows for joy in living but actually demands that what we do should be as perfect as possible, whether it be manual or artistic or intellectul work. The means are not narrowed down, neither are they to be called means so much as minor ends done for their own sake within an all-embracing end. I become more of a man when I am at liberty to think out an answer to a scientific problem, to concentrate on the perfection of a piece of sculpture or a novel, and the perfection asked for by the Christian ideal includes all that is human, being indeed the grace of it. Knowing this Dante could write that he saw within the depths of the "eternal light, bound by love in one volume, the scattered leaves of all the universe." But on the other hand where some definite end is sought, such as victory in a war, the return to prosperity of a nation, or the establishment of a Communist state, much has to be ruled out as unnecessary or harmful and everything which is kept is treated as a means to an immediate end, irrespective of its intrinsic value.

Christianity has been compared to an army on the march, but the image is more suited to communism. The former seeks allies, the latter is efficiently equipped to destroy the society through which it moves in order that it may rebuild a new one. The present is only a transitional stage, what Lenin called "Imperialism." The end, that of the classless society, may have to wait a long while. Whereas with Christianity the end is independent of time, communism puts it at a future date. In this respect, just as in the estimate of human values, communism is less accommodating and less wide in its sympathies. Those who live in the future perfect society will have all they want, but it will be at the expense of countless generations who have endured injustice and misery and been engaged in class struggles. This is not a bright or comforting view of life, and a suffering forerunner of the happy might well think that life was not worth the struggle. The age-long problems which have beset mankind, the vanity of the individual's effort, the purposeless suffering, the injustice which is never remedied, these have at times weighed so heavily on men and women as to lead to despair. Communism can only answer that the hecatomb of countless generations is necessary to bring about one future happy society. Christianity does not limit itself to some future event and sacrifice the present for its sake. The very name of gospel means "good news," and the news is intended for all mankind. The estrangement or alienation of man from God is to be overcome, and God himself, who cannot suffer defeat, is to be the means of overcoming it. This reconciliation is to take no account of Jew or barbarian, white or colored races, time or space; even those who lived before Christ are included, for all are reconciled and invited to the feast.

There is no mistaking the universality of the promise and the proclamation; but, it is sure to be said, this is only a façade; the reality is quite different. What Christianity gives with one hand, it takes away with the other, for in fact this good news is reserved for the few, for the Church, and the vast mass of mankind is left out and handed over to perdition. The Catholic Church, in particular, is suspected to be as intolerant and exclusive as communism. It does little for the vast majority of mankind in this world and gives them no hope for the next. It is relatively to the vast multitude of mankind a small sect, like a club in a city with strict rules of admission, with its dividends reserved for members only. But this is a caricature. The influence of Christianity extends far beyond its gates, and if it be, as it claims to be, the semblance of God himself represented in the countenance of God-made-man, it cannot possibly be a cheap and ready merchandise to be bought at every street corner. If it is a city set on a hill, which all can see, it must be a very high hill, and not one to be climbed without effort. In human estimate what is precious is rare—and what is rich as well as lovely—the St. Matthew Passion of Bach, the poetry of St. John of the Cross—needs time and discipline of spirit to be fully appreciated. The Christian Church is the witness of God and his promises; it is also the fruit of Christ's rejection, when he came to announce glad tidings, "Amen, amen, I say to you, before Abraham was, I am. They took up stones, therefore, to cast at him."

The comparative smallness of the Christian Church, therefore, is due to causes which do no discredit to it. If Christianity be human at all, it must abide by human conditions, and the consummate perfection of Christ, although he presented himself to the most religiously trained people in the world, was unrecognized. The means of perfection are still being offered and if the number of those who accept them be small, that reflects not upon Christianity so much as on those who having eyes will not see. And as to the masses of mankind, who have not darkened their minds to truth, they are not without hope or the benefit of Christianity. In the Christian message it is God who plans the reconciliation and happiness of mankind, and with him "all things are possible." No one can lose God's friendship except by his own fault, and it is commonly held that through the surpassing power of Christ and the co-operation of those who live in him, the multitudes, whether they lived in remote past ages or in the Christian dispensation, may attain the salvation promised by Christ. That seems to be suggested by the Pauline comparison that as all died in Adam, so all are brought to life in Christ. Christ is the new Adam, and more than an Adam, for "God has put all things in subjection under his feet, that is, all things have been made subject to him . . . and when that subjection is complete, then the Son himself will become subject to the power which made all things his subjects, so that God may be all in all." There is no limitation here, nor again in a parallel passage: "It was God's good pleasure to let all completeness dwell in him, and through him to win back all things, whether on earth or in heaven, into union with himself, making peace with them through his blood, shed on the cross." These last words show that in the expression "all things" St. Paul was thinking primarily of men and women, though he does not leave out in his mighty sweep nature itself, which in some strange way is to be reset so as to be conformed to the new unity of the whole world under Christ. In truth, then, the offering of the blessings brought by Christ is unrestricted.

These and many other passages show that, no matter how strict are the conditions of obeying the divine command to belong to the divine society founded by Christ, the gospel of hope is for the whole world. This was how the gospel was understood by many of the leading writers of the early centuries. St. Irenaeus, for instance, taught that, from the earliest times and everywhere, through the Word of God the revelation of the Fatherhood of God was obscurely but truly made known, so that he could be the "Salvation of those born outside the Way." The same kind of teaching can be found in St. Hilary, St. Ambrose, and in St. John Chrysostom, and the tenor of it is that no person since the dawn of man has lacked the means of "salvation." But the divine providence which leaves no one out works through the divine event, which, like the music of Orpheus, gathers both savage and human to its sound, that is, the advent of Christ; for I being lifted up "will draw all things to myself." Mankind has a mysterious unity, and by what may be called its "collective unconscious," * it adapts itself and responds to the still unknown and supernatural vocation of God. Christ, to use another image, descends into Hell. The Christian society, which is the extension of Christ in time and space, refashions the broken unity of mankind and forms a higher order. What Marx calls the dialectic of history is seen by the Christian as a conscious and unconscious striving towards a unity and order, the Vergilian story of men carrying their household gods and looking for a city and a home, moving onwards but meeting with frustration.

The Christian society gives a meaning and destination to this Odyssey of mankind. In a sense Christianity could not have existed without this vast and slow preparation, for the mark of human life is gradual growth, the stages of which cannot be anticipated. Just as in nature a long series of selections and survivals has preceded the emergence of the animal organism, and a dawdling infancy and adolescence have to be spent before a human being is wholly emancipated, so centuries had to pass before mankind was ripe for perfection and its fulfillment in Christ. That one needs must love the highest when one sees it is only a half truth. Those who lived in these centuries belong in some sense to what was to come and profit by the bonds

* This not too intelligible expression taken from Jung refers to a class of unconscious experiences common to all men and women, and they show a predisposition for and dark intimation of the Christian mysteries.

which connect them with the Christian society. In a subdued sense they can be called the foster parents of Christianity. The Church is the supreme unity within a larger unity of mankind; it calls itself catholic because its mission is to all without exception, and it enjoins on each of its members the duty of acting and praying as if the whole world rested on his shoulders. The bell for matins tolls, not for death nor for me, but for the inextricably woven fates of all mankind. All this is summed up by a writer on the Church in the words: "The whole world taken up by man and made one with his destiny—man in his turn, in the whole stupendous complexity of his history, taken up by the Church; the world made spiritual by man, and man consecrated by the Church; the Church, in fine, holy, spiritual, worldwide, like an immense ship laden with all the fruits of the earth, will enter upon eternity."

There can be no doubt that the message of Christ brought new hope to those who heard it. *"Une grande espérance a traversé la terre."* When the disciples of the Baptist came asking: "Art thou he who is to come?" Christ answered in messianic language: "Go and relate to John what you have heard and seen; the blind see, the lame walk, the lepers are made clean, the deaf hear, the dead rise again, to the poor the gospel is preached." The prophecy of Ezechiel is fulfilled: "Thus saith the Lord God to these bones: 'Behold I will send spirit into you and you shall live.'" Hope is given to the whole world by the news that God is one who cares for man as a Father, and, what is more, for each one individually. This dignity, which every individual has, is, as we have seen, the kernel of the philosophy which calls itself Christian. In this respect it is markedly different from the Communist. Christianity admits gradations in human societies based on the degrees of service to the community. He who gives most should be the most honored; but its basic principle is the equality of all in the sight of God. Other religions and other societies divide men into two classes; if it be not that of owner and slave it is the more esoteric and religious one of the initiates and the profane, the elect and the common herd, the bacchants and the wandbearers, or perhaps what is foreseen by James Burnham, the skilled manager and the workers. The Soviet régime is faced with a similar division of the party and the rest. Such a division may be justified as an interim necessity before the state withers away, but what is far more difficult to excuse is the subordination of all human life to a society which is yet to come. The problem which scandalizes all the genuine lovers of mankind is the apparent waste, and a waste accompanied with so much suffering and injustice. Knowing as we do so little of the states of mind in primitive communities we cannot be sure how far they were contented. With peoples and nations of whom we have records we are better off. There is an almost identical story of mixed joys and griefs. The griefs make the more lasting impression, the sad epitaphs on the tombs of children, the lamentations over misfortune, the cries against injustice, the hard lot of the slave and laborer, the inconstancy of love, the crying as of children in the night with no language but a cry. What hurts perhaps most is the feeling of loneliness and desertion and the experience of unjust treatment without any redress in this world. That human life, too, is an unfinished affair comes home to the friends of those whose promise is cut short, the originality of mind like unripened corn, the flash of personality flickering into darkness.

To all this a Communist has nothing to say; the chorus which sings that "Nothing is here for tears, nothing to wail or knock the breast" comes from another faith. The secularist is bound to see history as a process cyclical or evolutionary or dialectical; at best his eyes are on a future for which all generations must labor. Here is the irony of slaves building without reward the sepulchres of kings. The Christian assigns an imperishable reward to each single individual and generation. History is not so much a succession as a series of ultimate moments. In my beginning is my end; the ultimate is not far off. It is now. This is the eschatological teaching of the New Testament. What is now recognized in art is to be attributed, also, to every single human life. In art there is a process and perhaps an advance, and the nineteenth-century art world was beguiled by this. But greater knowledge and a wider appreciation of other civilizations have convinced us that great art is no respecter of time and can be found in all the nooks and crannies of history. The art of the Sung dynasty, of Nara and Gandhara, the mosaics of the Church of Kahrieh Djami in Constantinople, the Giotto frescoes in the Madonna dell' Arena chapel at Padua, all belong to different ages, but each has its own incomparable virtue. Art, however original, is not a special creation in the correct meaning of the word, as man is, no matter how defective or defaced a creation this or that individual may appear to be to his fellow men. The understanding of this and the compassion which springs from it is specifically Christian, as so many critics have noticed. In, for instance, the novel of Dostoevsky, Mitya Karamazov gives a typical example of this compassion, when he is accused of the murder of his father. He falls asleep and dreams, and his dream is not of himself, but of his driving through the steppes past a burning village, where the afflicted people are crying out to him. "And he felt that a passion of pity, such as he had never known before, was rising in his heart, that he wanted to cry, that he wanted to do something for them all, so that the babe should weep no more, so that the dark-faced dried-up mother should not weep, that no one should shed tears again from that moment. . . ." Such an attitude, even down to the words, comes straight out of the New Testament. "He will wipe away every tear from their eyes, and there will be no more death, or mourning, or cries of distress, no more sorrow; these old things have passed away." Whatever may appear to be the lot of the individual, and however insignificant his lifework in the opinion of his contemporaries, he is in the Christian belief what H. G. Wells called a prince in a slum, and his royalty is one day to be acclaimed.

The Communist view is, as already stated, that the hope offered by Christianity is an illusory one, which serves as a substitute for the earthly happiness which society has not so far provided. Although this objection has already been met, there remains the question to what extent Christianity promises happiness in this world or what is its attitude to social welfare and civilization. But as a prelude to this it will be convenient to discuss an accusation which is made against both communism and Christianity. They are both, it is said, authoritarian, and like all dictatorships they are intolerant and persecute dissenters when they can. They both have a sacred scripture, the Bible for the Christian, the Marxist writings for the Communist; neither allows any deviation from them. The Russian régime professes to be democratic and to be a lover of freedom, but Marxists put their own meaning on those words, and in truth I do not think that they mind being accused of intolerance. They are prepared to defend their deeds, and when they hide or deny facts the reason is lest their people, still infected with bourgeois ideas, should be scandalized, and the powerful world of their enemies combine against them. The end justifies the means. Their ethical code judges all by the far off boundary point. Nature is prolific and not squeamish; much perishes that the continuance of life may be assured; and man is part of nature. This is the scientific point of view, but the crusading Communist is on fire for social justice. Stalin wrote of the Marxist's "profound faith in the creative forces of the proletariat and in the revolutionary rightness of its class instinct." In this combination of scientific ruthlessness and moral élan, tolerance cannot find a place. It is an escapist or sentimental virtue.

On the principles and premises of communism intolerance and persecution are justified; the one worthwhile matter for deliberation is whether such means pay. If the Communist is wrong, it must be because his premises and presuppositions are false. Christianity, on the other hand, cannot fall back on an alien philosophy, and so ignore criticism of its methods and practice. The Christian is the first to denounce the intolerance of the Soviet rulers, their persecution of religion, of civilian opponents, and even their own innocent subjects. The Church has to be judged on its own principles, and there is no denying that its history contains dark pages. In the first centuries of its existence it was forced to be a *gens lucifuga* and learnt from the proscription of its worship by the Roman power and from the sufferings of its martyrs what persecution meant. Not till after the time of Constantine had it any say in the treatment of other religions or heretics. The age was not a soft one; nevertheless the great bishops of the time shrank from the use of force, their attitude being that of St. Athanasius that "it is the business of religion not to compel but to persuade." This spirit maintained itself during the period of the making of Christendom, and indeed the principle contained in the Christian philosophy was stated with admirable clarity by Alcuin, the Yorkshireman, who had been brought to the court of Charlemagne to be his literary counsellor. He protested against the policy of Charlemagne of offering the heathen Saxons the choice between baptism and death. "Faith is a matter of will, not of necessity. How can you force a man to believe what he does not believe? One can force baptism on people, but not faith. Man, an intelligent being, reasons; disposition, and desire for truth ought to bring him to recognize the truth of our holy faith. And prayer, above all, ought to bring down on him the mercy of Almighty God; for argument echoes in vain, if the dew of grace does not wet the heart of the hearer."

Here in this passage is the Christian insistence on the rights of a man as a person and a free person, but with the rise of the Christian states the Church became involved in their affairs and had to meet a situation in which all pointed to the need of severe measures of suppression. To understand the situation it must be remembered that at the time the Church felt itself greatly responsible for the morals as well as the faith of the peoples it had baptized, that bishops had far more to say in civil matters than now and were often ministers of state. In this situation princes and bishops were faced with a heresy which was also pernicious to the state, Catharism. The Cathari believed amongst other doctrines that sex was wrong and procreation a sin and that if a child were born it was right to starve it to death. They were a Gnostic sect hating all that was physical and so longing to be separated from the evil of the body that suicide was meritorious. As might be expected the result of such extreme puritanism was an outburst of licentiousness. The heresy, as can be seen, was both theological and social, and Church and state joined hands in the suppression of it. Once the Churchman moved on to this path he tended to lose sight of the principles which the earlier Christians had invoked. The temptation was strong. Manners were harsh and punishments at the time were savage, and though the Christian conscience was never stifled and protests were raised by saints, cities were put to the sword and prisoners often massacred. The fierce fanaticism of the Moors and Moslems stirred retaliation, and brought a decline instead of an advance in Christian manners. The close co-operation between the Christian religion and human societies has always been a danger to it. A purely spiritual religion with its eyes on the other world should be saved from worldliness and from taking on the characteristics of the society in which it lives; but Christianity is committed both to a superhuman end and to a participation in human affairs, and in its history the good and bad effects of this co-operation are clear to see. When the Communists accuse Christianity of being on the side of the capitalist they may at times be pointing to a real abuse, but they ignore its constant protection and defense of the poor and its constant warning to the rich.

Another reason which blinded the Church to the precepts contained in, for instance, the protest of Alcuin was the passionate belief in the necessity of the Christian faith for the ultimate happiness of every man. The Christian rulers tended to think in the simple terms that God himself had revealed the way and the truth; this revelation was so obviously true and so divinely important that a man, who twisted it in heresy or rejected it, must be in bad faith and culpable, and as culpable he deserved punishment. It would be treachery to God to be slack on this matter, especially as an offense against God in this matter was the greatest of all crimes. Such thinking obscures other counterbalancing doctrines, such as the rights of personality and the freedom which is the inalienable property of a person. The passion for righteousness and zeal for one's neighbor turns into a fanaticism. That this happened is well known, and there is no need to dwell on the persecutions by both Catholics and Protestants and the ugly spectacle of the religious wars. They arose out of an excess of belief, and stand out in contrast to the indifferentism which has succeeded them. But as soon as passionate political and national beliefs again emerged, the same kind of violence manifested itself, so that the last forty years have witnessed violence and persecution surpassing those of the past ages.

The resurgence of brutal persecutions has made the democratic peoples very sensitive to the dangers of intolerance and they look askance at examples of the former behavior of Christian bodies and at the story of the Inquisition. Some wonder whether there is anything to choose between the attitudes of Christianity and communism. There are amongst Christians themselves not a few who repudiate all forms of intolerance and force as out of harmony, as they say, with the Sermon on the Mount. Such an attitude is not borne out by other sayings and incidents in the Gospels. To get the right perspective it is necessary to distinguish between intolerance and the resort to physical force and also to keep a sense of history. At Oxford in past days the University exercised the power of life and death over students: in schools during the nineteenth century corporal punishment to our eyes brutal was administered day in day out. In Anglo-Saxon monasteries monks who sneezed during office were punished with a bread and water diet for days. It is, therefore, hardly to be expected that the Church, in days when corporal penalties were as much taken for granted as the eating of leeks by Welshmen, would have a twentieth-century mentality. Its mercy was active; it promoted works of mercy, and time and again advocated and practiced forgiveness of injuries, but it had not yet separated the vindication of justice and truth from forcible means. There are some nowadays who criticize the giving of rewards for merit. A time may come when such a practice will be thought primitive and unwholesome.

The fact, therefore, that in former and rougher times Christians persecuted religious enemies cannot be made a matter of comparison with the present-day methods of communism. But this is not, perhaps, the tender spot in the relations of the Church with the modern democratic societies; what is feared is that the Church, if it had its will, would not permit liberty to those of other faiths, or liberty of thought. The problem is how can the Church on its own principles condone a religion or the exercise of an opinion which it considers evil or dangerous. Let it be said that this problem as such is one which must trouble any society which values its own beliefs. The Church is made an object of attack because it puts a unique value on its beliefs and is thought to be more intransigent and narrower than other bodies. Even the most liberal minded ought to draw the line somewhere, and there is no state which does not draw up statutes protecting its citizens against anarchical and antinomian propaganda. Censorship is in force against certain kinds of obscenity in films and plays and books, and laws have become increasingly severe against Communist infiltration. In respect of the tolerance of other faiths the Church puts into use two principles which originate from its philosophy; one is that for the sake of the common good of a society and its peace much can be tolerated which in the abstract is against the Christian ideal. The modern state found that peace and order can be secured better by the ventilation of opinions than by the suppression of them, and this freedom promotes the general good, or at least that of the majority. This principle was invoked by Pope Pius XII in 1954 when he said that "in certain circumstances God does not give men any mandate, does not impose any duty, and does not even communicate the right to impede or to redress what is erroneous and false," and therefore where there are members of a state who hold certain religious views to be right "the free exercise" of their belief is permissible on Catholic principles. Not only the general good calls for such tolerance; the principle of the individual's freedom also operates. Liberty, which has taken on a new lease of life with the threat of the totalitarian state so close, is in its proper meaning an ideal for which Christianity has always stood, and now the Church itself invokes it on behalf of the rights of parents to choose the schools for their children; it fights, also, in atheist or secularist states for the right and liberty to worship. As liberty is rightly held in such high regard, the liberties of those who differ in religion from the Church must be respected, and it is safe to say that the whole climate of opinion owing to the emergence of these two principles has changed since the days of intolerance and religious warfare.

Just as the theory and practice of authority in Christianity differs from that of the Communist, so, as might be expected, does the concept of freedom. A materialist view of man and history seems to leave no room for freedom, but the Marxist makes great play of the idea, and is able to fit it into his system to the satisfaction of Communists. Freedom, as already noted, is defined by Marx as the knowledge of necessity. This pale description, which would tell us nothing about the meaning of freedom unless we knew already to what it referred, has to be seen against the backcloth of the Hegelian system. The Hegelian idea, too, has a very long ancestry, as it is to be found in most of the systems of thought or religion which are monistic or pantheistic. The clue is this, that the individual, who at first finds himself alone and moved about like a leaf in an alien universe, comes in the end to identify himself with the universe and to know himself as sharing in the movement or creativity of that universe. As a simple illustration take a slave in a society; he becomes emancipated, and this is the first step in freedom; but still he feels himself an individual inside a community which forces him to do this or that, and makes use of him; then in time he comes to identify himself with his community and to think of its action as his and of his as one with it; his private and small identity is being lifted up into a larger whole, where finally in the general will his will is included and he is now willing and thinking and at one with the community. Nothing now is outside or thwarting his will, and he has become for the first time fully free. This description holds true for those systems of thought which put Mind as the begetter of the universe and claim that an individual, when he loses the limitation of individuality and is made one with Mind itself, is fully free. Change the word mind to that of God, and we can see that the mystic and the poet are working out a not too dissimilar idea when they speak of conformity with the will of God, and say that "in His will is our peace." In fact, however, the idea of conformity with or adhesion to the will of God is notably different in that the individual never loses his personality so as to be one with Mind or nature in the sense meant by the monist or pantheist. From this, it is hoped, will be seen the value to Marx of the Hegelion idea of freedom. Necessity need no longer be an obstacle to freedom; it is the truth, rather, that in necessity real freedom is found, on condition that the connection between the two is realized.

In an idealistic system the connection between necessity and freedom may appear illuminating, though it would be better to use the word spontaneous or voluntary in place of free. An organism performs many actions which appear to be purposive and even selective; but in the absence of consciousness few would call the actions free. If these organic acts are accompanied with consciousness and if the conscious being enjoys these actions and concurs with them, the action can be called spontaneous, but in the absence of real choice, it does not deserve the name of freedom. There is one exceptional case, however, where the voluntary act does deserve the name of freedom. It might be that one loved so truly and well the person of one's choice that the whole self became absorbed in loving, and no other person could be thought worth considering! Here owing to the absence of competition, there would be no choice in the end, and yet the act is supremely free. There is no compulsion from without and one wills what one is doing with one's whole heart. Such a love, however, is not at first sight. Love at first sight blinds, and therefore is not complete. Complete love, as a rule, follows on a number of choices and is their culmination.

Now the trouble with the Marxist use of necessary freedom is that it does not fit into any of the above categories. Marx has taken over what looks plausible when applied to the meeting of mind with mind. Where material reality is all in all, it is difficult to see how mind can be free in surrendering itself to material surroundings, unless surreptitiously another meaning to freedom be introduced. A smaller mind being taken up into a greater one, consciousness identifying itself with the consciousness which designed or constructed nature and the individual mind itself, such a theory may sound possible and attractive. What is very hard to understand is how a mind, which is material at bottom, by knowing that it is material and subject to the same laws as matter, can thereby become free. What Marx is thinking of is plain and in part admirable; it is a truth which is valuable both in education and in psychology. It comes to this that we can exercise our freedom best when we know what we are up against. A savage is full of superstitious fears of nature, and uses magic to control the unknown forces; we get rid of these superstitions the more we know of the laws which govern nature, and through that knowledge we are able to use them and control them to our benefit. In psychology there is the well-known principle of facing reality. Many of our phobias and obsessions come from our fancies and from the unwillingness to look at the truth. To recognize that freedom is so closely associated with truth is expedient and valuable. Religious writers know this truth in terms of emancipation; the truth will set you free; the spiritual teachers of Islam and of Zen Buddhism, to take only two examples, inculcate a way and a technique, which, they claim, emancipates the self from its errors and limitations. The Christian writers all agree that the self can by understanding and practice of the truth be freed from the slavery of the passions and the longing for riches and material possessions. Communists have not shown any desire to be free of material possessions, nor did Marx expressly include among his freedoms the liberty of the spirit, but he did esteem the liberty which knowledge of nature can bring.

How this liberty is compatible with materialism is explained by Communist writers in a way which shows that they are sensitive to the difficulties to which their philosophy exposes them. Thus we are told that "although ideas can only arise from material conditions, when they do arise they certainly exert an influence on men's actions and therefore on the course of things. . . . The Marxist conception of social development (known as 'historical materialism') is therefore not a materialist 'determinism'—the theory that man's actions are absolutely determined by the material world round him. On the contrary, man's actions, and the material changes which these actions bring about, are the product partly of the material world outside him, and partly of his own knowledge of how to control the material world." (*What is Marxism?* by Emile Burns, p. 15.) In a primer of Marxism we are told that "unlike materialism, dialectical materialism, while stressing that matter is real and primary, also recognizes that thinking is something *new* which arises in the development of matter." Engels, who was probably the most intellectual of the early Marxists, was clearly uneasy on this matter of freedom. He owned in a letter to Bloch that he and Marx had been forced to exaggerate the part played in history by economic factors. They were forced to do this because the current philosophies, when they first wrote, ignored these factors. They never meant to deny that there were other factors as well. Conscious of this defect Engels often uses a language with which all, materialist or nonmaterialist, could agree. He says that ignorance hampers freedom, that "freedom of the will means nothing but the capacity to make decisions with real knowledge of the subject"; that "man has to make his own history, though he has not yet done so." Such sentences, except for the clause in the last one, look unexceptionable even to a Christian thinker, and they are comforting in this that they leave to the individual freedom of action despite the influence of natural causes. But this is done by equiparating "knowledge of necessity" with the power of acting upon nature, controlling and directing it, and clearly the two are not the same.

The Marxist defends his position by saying that in his view knowledge and action go together, and he adds that in dialectical materialism thought and matter interact and both produce effects. Such a defense, however, begs the question, for knowledge, if it is meant to be taken in its proper sense, and in a sense in which the Marxist constantly is bound to use it, does not act. The very definition given by Engels distinguishes between knowledge and will in the way we all do: "Freedom of the will means nothing but the capacity to make decisions with real knowledge of the subject." Here the making of decisions follows on true knowledge. I leave out the extra difficulty that knowledge is in Lenin's account only an aspect of matter or image of it. An image could not change nature; all it can do is to reflect it or the sense data or the sense impressions. The pathway gets darker and darker the further we pursue this extreme empiricist and materialistic philosophy. Engels admits that there are other factors than the economic one. We are not told what they are, and it is important to know. Whence comes this power to be able to stand free of the physical and economic and, I suppose, the psycho-physical causes? If I am free from them I am according to traditional philosophy a self-determined being, and as such I am truly free, but I am also a spiritual being. A spiritual being is one who can conceive an end which is not caused, so to speak, from behind. The mind instead of being pushed looks ahead, and in the light of conflicting ends is able to choose which it will pursue; in this sense it is self-determining and not material. The Marxist willy-nilly has to grant this because the human being having "the capacity to make decisions with real knowledge of the subject" does according to him direct society to the end for which man is properly suited, that is, the classless society. But this is an admission of the old teleological notion, of the capacity of man to conceive of an end which is not yet existing and to plan his actions to achieve it; and this again is precisely what proves that man is more than a material being.

The Christian conception of freedom starts at this very point where the Marxist blacks out. What the

Marxist says of man is almost true, but not quite. The scientific calculations of his behavior are of great utility, but they are never certain. The Christian philosopher has often more sympathy with the materialistic view than with the idealistic or exclusively rational. We are in so many respects a part of nature; our bodies obey chemical and physical laws. Our powers are limited to a tiny field of action, and that field can be further limited by illness or psychopathical failings. Our brains can be washed, our habits conditioned, and there is a breaking point when we must surrender or collapse. Our heredity, our environment, physical and human, provide the raw material on which our will has to work; so much so that it is common to exaggerate and say that our particular desires and sentiments and emotional responses and interests are what they are because of place and time and company. Of all this we are only too aware, and at times we are tempted to give up the struggle to change the unlovable features of our character. How much we can change them is always a matter of uncertainty; the fact is that we attain a degree of mastery over ourselves and we can unify what is in us in the pursuit of some ideal. Statistics and mass observation may show that on the average men and women will react in a settled way to hunger, to sex, to fear and luxury, and public opinion. Predictions of this kind are not the same as scientific prediction, and even were they scientific, in the sense of accurate, there would still be room for freedom; for we could never be sure that some persons had not freely acted in the way predicted.

The Christian philosophy of man favors a theory of

the closest interaction between mind and body, spirit and matter; and consequently the discoveries of medicine and biology are cheerfully greeted with "I told you so." But the truth lies in this interaction, and not in the denial of one of the agents or in the confusion of the two under one concept. This is where the Marxist and the Christian part company, at the point, that is, where Engels seems to hesitate. Human consciousness is not just a luminous glow given off by the body or a mere reflection of physical behavior. The property of the mind which cannot be explained in material terms is its power both to have knowledge of what is happening and why it is happening and by means of universal concepts, and also to be aware of what it is doing at the same moment. Consciousness is also self-consciousness, and this double operation of the mind has no counterpart in nature and no physical basis. In this operation we are both thinking and watching our thinking, acting and aware of how and why we are acting; we stand off our own selves to that degree of detachment which enables us to judge the impulses and motives which are inciting us and say "this is what I ought to do and this is what I want to do"; and unless we are carried away by one of the impulses we are able to judge them by a standard, which may be absolute. A prisoner of the Gestapo or the Politburo, for instance, can, until his manhood and freedom are destroyed, refuse to tell lies about his friends and betray his country. In so doing he is holding to an absolute standard of truth and loyalty. This power comes from his being a person, one who is able to determine himself and have responsibility and liberty of thought and action, and this is the same as saying that a person is spirit as well as matter, and has his ultimate destiny in a world where spiritual perfection, the perfection, that is, of knowledge and love, can be attained.

The Communist and the Christian are both devoted to a cause, and in practice both they and their leaders assume free will. They lead, and encourage, and call for loyalty and sacrifice. The chief virtues of proletarian morality should be, according to Kalinin, love of one's own people, of the working classes, uprightness . . . avoidance of lying and deceit, seemly behavior, courage, comradeship, and love of work. These virtues spring naturally to his mind when he asks the best from his Communist friends, and they are the virtues which only those who dedicate themselves to an ideal can make their own. They need not, however, be exercised towards those outside the pale of communism, for, as we have seen, all means are fair in the warfare with those who stand in the way of the Soviet Socialist order. The Christian is taught to practice the same virtues, but above all to show "charity to all men" without exception. Each person has been made in the likeness of God, and by the exercise of his freedom he has to try to "be perfect even as your heavenly Father is perfect." This means a constant strife with oneself and constant love for one's neighbor. The inward strife consists in subduing the barbarian in oneself, in fighting against meanness, selfishness, and hate. Freedom is essential for self-development and is its crown. But enlightened self-interest is not the ideal. Hope for a free society living in peace and concord is part of the ideal, though even such a society is only the image of a more perfect and perpetual society, where God is all in all.

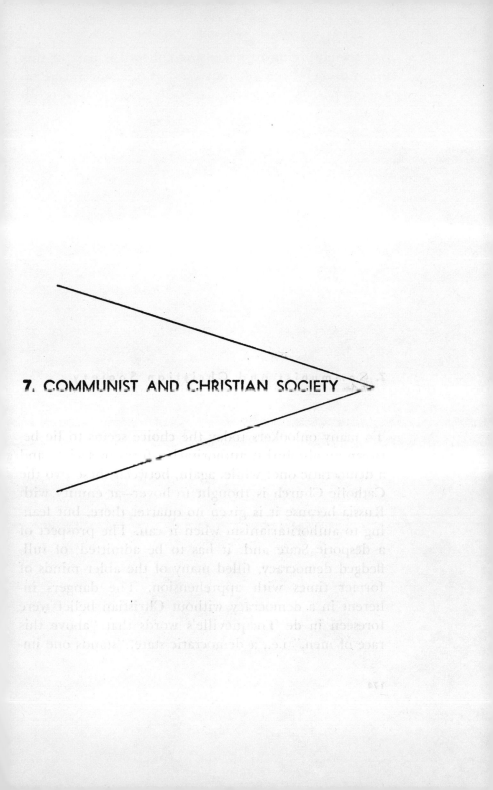

7. COMMUNIST AND CHRISTIAN SOCIETY

7. Communist and Christian Society

To many onlookers today the choice seems to lie between an absolutist, authoritarian form of society and
a democratic one; while, again, between these two the
Catholic Church is thought to hover—at enmity with
Russia because it is given no quarter there, but leaning to authoritarianism when it can. The prospect of
a despotic State and, it has to be admitted, of full-
fledged democracy, filled many of the abler minds of
former times with apprehension. The dangers inherent in a democracy without Christian belief were
foreseen in de Tocqueville's words that "above this
race of men," i.e., a democratic state, "stands one im-

mense and tutelary power, which takes upon itself alone to secure their gratifications and to watch over their fate. That power is absolute, minute, regular, provident, and mild; . . . it provides for their (the people's) security, foresees and supplies their necessities, facilitates their pleasures, manages their principal concerns, directs their industry, regulates the descent of property, and subdivides their inheritances— what remains but to spare them all the care of thinking and all the trouble of living?" Burckhardt was pessimistic about the future of the workers of the world, and what he writes has a special application to Russia: "There is a curious future in store for the workers. I have a vision which may look quite foolish at present, but I cannot get rid of it: the militarized state must become a mass manufacturer. These human agglomerations in the workshops cannot be left in all eternity to their despair and envy: what, quite logically, should be introduced is a certain controlled degree of misery with promotions and uniforms, started and concluded every day under the beating of drums." Still more direct are the words of Constantine Leontyev. "Russian society, which is already egalitarian in its customs, will be dragged more rapidly than other societies along the fatal road of general confusion. And who knows whether, like the Jews who unexpectedly produced the teacher of a new faith, we shall not suddenly give birth to Antichrist? He will spring from the bowels of our political system, which will cast off all class distinctions, and then all vestige of an ecclesiastical principle."

Marx, as can be seen, is not the only prophet of the future, and critics, who are not of his faith, on looking at the course which Lenin and Stalin have followed, tend to side with Burckhardt, Leontyev, de Custine, de Tocqueville, and others. Whereas Lenin described the period after the Russian collapse as an interim preluding the peace of the classless society, critics protest that they see no sign of freedom for the workers, land to the peasants and liberty to the suppressed nationalities. Lenin gained power by force and did not hesitate to crush all who stood in the way of his ideas. His successor increased the control over the factory workers and the villagers. The Orthodox Church was humbled, and science, literature, and art were subjected to the directives of the new régime. Citizens found themselves without a voice of their own in the government as the trade unions came to be subjected to members of the Party, and the peoples of the small republics, such as the Trans-Caucasian and the Ukraine, were brought under the central authority in Moscow. Representation gradually became a matter of form and opportunities for it happened more and more rarely, and even Party Congresses were in time superseded by the dictatorship of one man. The strictest surveillance has been exercised on workers and intellectuals, and when they deviate from orthodoxy members of the Party are deprived of their party card, while those not of the Party disappear. Finally, to make sure of the purity of the Marxist faith and in order to keep authority intact, Stalin in the great purge made away with thousands of suspects including some of those who had been staunch comrades of Lenin and had borne with him the heat of the struggle in its critical days.

Even those sympathetic with Marxist ideals have found this record a stumbling block. To the neutral historian it looks not like a confirmation of Marxist predictions so much as a repetition of a well-known rhythm in historical revolutions. A tocsin is sounded, a banner is waved, the hopes of the people are stirred, and then a group begins to exploit the hopes of the masses. The group breaks up into factions, and the strong man emerges, who exterminates his rivals and then rules the people with a rod of iron. Let it be said, however, that in time, some at least of the ideas, which excited the hopes of the multitudes, win through and become part of the new order. Stalin and his successors have not, as we know, accepted this interpretation. Their answer is that all is going according to plan, that is according to the Marxist formula. The conditions in Russia, its iron discipline, its secretiveness and its militarism, are forced upon it by the unscrupulous behavior and propaganda of its enemies. There is no other road to the classless society than by the means adopted, and in the meanwhile the Russian state has begun what is true democracy. It has changed the status of the workers; the party and the leaders are acting all the time in the interest of the people, and the proof lies in the extraordinary successes in every line of production, the improvement in the education of the proletariat and the application of science to perfect the material conditions of life. The present system of control and dictatorship is only a passing phenomenon, the narrow gate which leads to perfection.

For those who are convinced that Marx has arrived at the final truth about man and nature and that his philosophy of history is scientifically certain, this answer must seem satisfactory. What is happening has a certain inevitability about it. To those, however, who are less dogmatic about man and draw their lessons from the past and from what they know of the dangers of power, the trend of events in Russia and in the satellite countries does look more like the usual corrupt influence of power on those who have been given it and have increased it. The gap between the freedom of the people and the government should surely show signs of diminishing, whereas during the rule of Stalin it so increased as to resemble the ancient slave state. The following passage by Ladislas Rieger, the Professor of Philosophy at Prague, therefore, will strike a Communist as sober truth, and others as rhetoric: "We are struggling for the most perfect government of, by, and for the people, for a socialist democracy in which our children can live as citizens liberated from all terror and oppression and in which there will be no exploitation, no human degradation in subservience to wealth and capital. . . . A new Man will arise, the ruler of the earth, and, in the atomic age, perhaps even the ruler of other planets—the ruler of a new history the curve of which will continuously rise toward higher degrees of spiritual and material civilization, thus overcoming all lower stages in harmony with the cosmic dialectics of being" (*Democracy in a World of Tensions*, p. 273, edited by Richard McKeon).

Criticisms by those who are not Communist are treated by Marxists as necessarily prejudiced. They are inherently dishonest because they are the outcome of a capitalist ideology. The Christian is, therefore, disarmed from the start. He is besides held in special contempt because he makes such high pretences and is nothing but a hanger-on of the oppressors of the people. This charge is made by others than Communists, and there are also Christians who bend over backward to accuse themselves and the Christian bodies of laziness, sycophancy and, like the Pharisees, of putting burdens on others' shoulders. Christianity has had a long history, and during it it has laid itself open to these kinds of accusation. To keep to more recent history, in some countries the Churches have suffered from too close an alliance with the state, and Church officials have acted almost as lackeys. In Russia the Orthodox Church was said to be too political, the Catholic Church in Austro-Hungary to be a mere department of the state, and in England in the eighteenth century Anglicanism so lost touch with the people that Wesley found an immense and neglected field ready for his mission. Hence an Anglican writer can say that "it must be granted that the Marxist critique is true of a great deal of religion, and in particular of a great deal of nineteenth-century religion," though he does not make his case stronger by adding that "high churchmanship replaced social eminence as the mark of the staunch Anglican. The ascetic discipline which the Tractarians commended was of a kind possible only to a leisured class: their sacramental doctrines were irrelevant in the industrial situation." As if St. Francis of Assisi had been an ascetic member of the leisured class, and Don Bosco had given up the sacraments!

Christians may well be censured for not having done

more to keep religion alive among the masses, and for having accepted too easily as an act of God their poverty and unfair conditions; they may have been out of date in their methods of apostleship. From the time of the Apostles members, and leading members, have been asleep when Christ has been in agony. But a lazy doctor, even an unskilful one, does not thereby discredit all medicine, and Christianity has never said that it was composed of saints. Its one claim is that it has the remedy and the hope of the world in its keeping. To be fair, too, Christianity has never ceased to be concerned with the poor and to fight against injustice. There has been a continuous stream of men and women who have given up their lives to helping those less fortunate than themselves, to tending the sick, looking after orphans, the lame and the blind and the outcasts of society. They have fought for legislation to end inequalities of race and color and class, and they have set an example in their own lives of what Christianity is meant to be. A man like St. Vincent de Paul is unusual only by the extraordinary number of his good works. He managed in his lifetime to take up the cause of sailors, tramps, invalid workmen, agricultural laborers, to found institutes for the clergy, schools for the poor, and congregations such as the Sisters of Charity. More recently still, as social problems became the question of the time, Pope Leo XIII and his successors Pius XI and Pius XII issued a series of letters in which the principles which must govern the social relations of man with man, worker with employer and citizens with the state were laid down, forming a Christian workman's charter, which may well be compared with the Manifesto of Marx.

Soviet writers, therefore, are not fair to Christianity when they deny its interest in the poor and ignore its many heroic efforts to help them and raise their condition of life. Their case rests really on different grounds, of which the chief is that Christian charity is a form of condescension, that of Dives giving an alms to Lazarus. Such charity is considered a denial of democracy and the principle of equality. On this last point the socialist democrats of the English-speaking countries are disposed to agree with the Communists. They view the Catholic Church especially with doubting eyes. It may be the enemy of communism, but to what extent are its principles consistent with democracy? Thus Dr. Matthew B. Lucas, for instance, writing in a composite volume, *Religious Faith and World Culture,* says that "the religious institutions of Christendom have been, for the most part, highly undemocratic in practice. With few exceptions they have propagated exclusive and authoritarian dogma in an atmosphere of obscurantism, and even terrorism, better suited to the fanatical ideologies of totalitarian powers than to the channels of spiritual grace."

To democrats such as Dr. Lucas the rock of offense is authoritarianism, and from the days of its Founder Christianity has spoken "as one having authority." Authority now has the effect of an icy wind because of its associations with Fascism, Nazism and the totalitarian powers. This is unfortunate because no state or society can exist without some authority, and the Christian is prepared to argue that without the understanding of its proper meaning and the exercise of proper authority the world is bound to suffer under despotisms, whether they be single dictatorships or so-called democratic régimes. Every society must have a government to carry out what is necessary for its continuity and welfare, and it cannot do that without the power and the authority. A democracy believes that it chooses a government, which will represent its wishes, so that it will be by the people, for the people and with the people. But in fact the means of controlling a government are always limited. As Bertrand Russell remarked in his Reith Lectures: "You have, it is true, a twenty-millionth share in the government of others, but only a twenty-millionth share in the government of yourself. You are therefore much more conscious of being governed than of governing." A state and a government is not likely to use power rightly unless the rulers have a conscience and are directed by moral law. The Christian philosophy of authority is that both in the family and in the state the authority is a moral one, to which obedience is due, and this authority in the state, however conferred, is derived from God, the fountain of Justice. Who mentions God mentions authority because he is the creater of man and created him to live in accordance with his will and in a community, where each helps the other. Without God authority becomes arbitrary power. Its sanction has been removed. In Dostoevsky's *The Possessed* there is a passage which excellently illustrates this. " 'As a matter of fact,' Shatov declared, 'if there is a revolution in Russia, it will have to start with the propagation of atheism.' An old, tough captain with gray hair sat and sat in silence, and did not breathe a word. All of a sudden he rose in the very middle of the room and, you know, said aloud just as if speaking to himself: 'If there is no God how can I then be a captain?' He took his cap, threw up his hands and left."

This account may seem to some platitudinous and to others to leave out the crucial point in authority, namely, the right to command with the corresponding duty of obedience. For some time the liberalistic political theories have minimized the notion of sovereign power in a state, and in modern times the positivists have left it out entirely. The key to the Christian view is belief in the existence of God. Most men and women, in practice, recognize some moral rights and duties in the family and in the state and are scandalized when children flaunt the orders of their parents, or when citizens deliberately break the law. The Christian position is that both the family and the state have their authority from God, because to live the life intended by God the family and the state are essential. For that reason they are said to have a moral and not merely conventional or legal authority. God created man, and human life is called the natural order; God also instituted the Christian Church, and what belongs to that is called the supernatural order.

To take this latter first. Newman, when still an Anglican in 1842, in a sermon called "The Christian Church an Imperial Power," insisted that Christianity by its very nature and from the beginning took on an authoritative character. He cited the prophecies in the Old Testament from Isaiah and Daniel and the Psalms and pointed out that the note of kingship pervades the Gospels. Out of Bethlehem "shall he come forth unto Me, that is to be the Ruler in Israel." Of the promise made to St. Peter he writes that "by the Church must be meant a community or polity of men, and you see that St. Peter had the keys of this Church or kingdom, or the power of admitting into it, and excluding from it: and besides that, an awful power of binding and loosing, about which it does not fall within our present subject to inquire." At the end Newman sums up by saying that "if we will be Scriptural in our view of the Church, we must consider that it is a kingdom, that its officers have great powers and high gifts, that they are charged with the custody of Divine Truth, and they are all united together, and that the nations are subject to them. If we reject this kind of ministry, as inapplicable to the present day, we shall in vain go to Scripture to find another. If we will form to ourselves a ministry and a Church bereft of the august power which I have mentioned, it will be one of our own devising; and let us pretend no more to draw our religion from the Bible. Rather we are like Jeroboam who made his own religion." If this be right then the office of ruling is inherent in the Christian Church, as it is in all civil societies. But it is above all most requisite and determined in the Church because it is concerned with the chief end of man, and the way has been shown and ordained by God himself. That is why the authority of the Church is said to be plenary. It has the authority to teach and to sanctify, and it also has jurisdiction. A governing body in a sovereign state has jurisdiction, and this includes the right to pass laws, to judge, and to coerce; and this

184

plenary power must be distinguished from that of other societies such as the family or a particular association. These latter have no more than what has been described as an authority of dominion; that is, they can command and punish, but their judicial powers are curtailed, and they cannot issue legislation binding on the community in perpetuity.

The Christian Church bases its authority on a commission from God; its end is the everlasting happiness of its members, but as a visible society it has to exercise authority on visible members, and also to coexist with other civil societies whose end is the welfare of their citizens. Within its own realm its authority is absolute, but from this it must not be straightway inferred that its régime and methods are like those of a totalitarian or despotic civil power. Its sanctions are mainly spiritual, such as deprivation of the sacraments or excommunication, and its presiding end is charity. What separates it, however, most decisively from the Fascist or Communist authoritarianism is the freedom given to the individual to enter into it and to depart from it unmolested. If a man were to decide that he did not believe in the Church or did not approve of its rule, all he has to do is to cease to practice the religion. If he remain a member, it is because he is a willing member and believes in the truth of the organization. This constantly forgotten fact, which gives a sense to spiritual authority quite different from that of the totalitarian state, has been excellently put as follows. "The highly developed exterior organization that wins our admiration is but an expression, in accordance with the needs of this present life, of the interior unity of a living entity, so that the Catholic is not only the subject of a power but is a member of a body as well, and his legal dependence on this power is to the end that he may have part in the life of the body. His submission in consequence is not an abdication, his orthodoxy is not mere conformity, but fidelity. It is his duty not merely to obey her orders or show deference to her counsels, but to share in a life, to enjoy a spiritual union." This has to be borne in mind even when critics find justifiable reason for irritation with the tone and manner of Catholics in office. There is no guarantee in the Catholic Church that those in authority will be free from the weaknesses which so often accompany the assumption of power. Much depends upon times and circumstances. In most modern governments, with the perhaps inevitable increase of bureaucracy, the inhuman and the bullying type of official has multiplied as never before. Even those holding a spiritual office may be likewise affected, but there is a strong reason why Churchmen invested with authority should not be harsh and dominating, seeing that the basic doctrine of authority for Christians is given in the words of Christ: "The kings of the gentiles lord it over them, . . . but you not so; he that is the greater among you, let him become as the younger; and he that is the leader, as he that serveth."

It is not then primarily as a human institution that the Church continues to be dogmatic and authoritarian. If God does, as it claims, speak through it it is bound to speak with authority and certainty on those matters on which it is the voice and the custodian. But even human institutions, as we have seen, forswear divine authority at their peril. As Dr. Dwight J. Bradley has written: "The classical concept of authority cannot survive indefinitely the loss of its major premise: the existence of an authoritative God. When the premise is abandoned the logical sequence is to deal with, and perhaps to appease, every situation in an expediently relative way, and to take from life's conflicting issues their distinctly rational and moral gravity." This generalization is not an arbitrary one. The presence and acceptance of a religious creed which keeps ever before the mind the idea of a God who is the fountain of justice and the final arbiter of life did, in fact, in past ages give majesty to the Common Law and to the judicial systems of England and the United States. Obedience to constituted authority seems both rational and virtuous. But the rational basis subsided when the Christian dogmas were put away in the lumber room. What Patmore said of love, that "it is sure to be something less than human if it is not something more," can be applied also to morals and authority. Deprived of a firm religion which draws back the curtain of eternity, morality becomes a creature of the day and seems to be continually varying its hue in the shadows and in the sunlight. In the modern secular state there has been a tendency to seek for the basis of authority in the general goodness of man as expressed in the will of the state, in the greatest happiness of the greatest number or in the expediency of positive law. The voice of the multitude has come more and more to be accepted as the ultimate sanction, and the very mention of authority causes a protest from those who have banked on individual liberty. But authority may be driven out of doors, yet it always returns and, if it be not welcome in its rightful dress, it comes dressed in absolute power and without any regard for persons. In the modern state authority hides behind multiple regulations and petty officials. It is impersonal but not despotic as in the totalitarian states. There economic materialism wedded to the dictatorship of the proletariat gives birth to a demonic authoritarianism. It takes the place of the old authority, which, with its religious dogmas, provided a charter for the liberties of the spirit, and binds the individual in a gauntlet of steel and makes him subject to a ruthless domination.

Where Christianity was acknowledged in many states, as in Europe in the Middle Ages, there also the state was prevented from assuming an omnipotence and a complete control over its subjects. When the unity of Christendom was broken the state tended to take over spiritual authority as well. But in so doing it challenged the long-thought-out Christian theory of the state. That such a theory exists is now almost forgotten. It was restated by Pope Leo XIII in clear terms. "Man's natural instinct moves him to live in civil society, for he cannot, if dwelling apart, provide himself with the necessary requirements of life, nor procure the means of developing his mental and moral faculties. Hence it is divinely ordained that he should lead his life—be it family, social, or civil—with his fellow men, amongst whom alone his several wants can be adequately supplied. But as no society can hold together unless some one be over all, directing all to strive earnestly for the common good, every civilized community must have a ruling authority, and this authority, no less than society itself, has its source in nature, and has, consequently, God for its author. Hence it follows that all public power must proceed from God: for God alone is the true and supreme Lord of the world. Everything, without exception, must be subject to him, and must serve him, so that whosoever holds the right to govern holds it from one sole and single source, namely God the Sovereign Ruler of all. There is no power but from God." The moral ground of authority, absent in so many modern theories, is very marked in this passage. It should be noted, however, that the constant reference back to God does not affect the commonly held view that authority comes from the people. The point is that if the sovereignty of the ruler is dependent upon the will of the people, that sovereignty once constituted derives its moral right to command and calls for the moral obedience of the subjects because it ultimately descends from God. The right to rule is not necessarily bound up with any special mode of government, provided only that it be of a nature to insure the general welfare. The same Pope goes on to say that "they who rule should rule with even-handed justice, not as masters, but rather as fathers. . . . Government should moreover be administered for the well-being of the citizens, because they who govern others possess authority solely for the welfare of the state." This government may be kingly or oligarchic or republican. Nowadays it is taken for granted that democracy is the only genuine form of government which gives room for the exercise of liberty and is government for the people. As all authority is given for the sake of the community, it is not clear that democracy, as understood today, can claim to be the only rightful form of government. Indeed, in so far as it takes over the divine prerogative and assigns it to the people, it is moving away from the Christian conception. The Christian idea is not the same as that of Rousseau. Rousseau's ultimate is the sovereign people. In his theory there is an original happy state of nature with innocent man dwelling in it; the more these people are given liberty the better they will be, and nothing better can be thought of than to consult their wishes. Hence the dogma of the general will and the divinization of numbers. We are left with untrammelled freedom and a general will, the difficulty of knowing what the general will is and extracting moral authority and moral duties out of it! Faced with this problem Kant decided that the individual, as a rational being, must obey a law which is rational, and that condition must be found in the state. This, as Morris in his *History of Political Ideas* says, formulated itself finally for Kant and for Hegel in the question: Is there any Being to whom I can say, "Whatever you order, I feel obliged to obey?" And the answer is, the State or nothing. To Kant the only law strictly binding is one I make myself, one in which I make and realize the Realm of Reason —Law. For Hegel the realm of reason is not only in process of being realized; it must be at every moment also actual and real, and "the march of God upon earth" can be found in its real unity and in its highest expression only in the State. The transfer of the march of reason to the materialist dialectic of history has already been discussed. What now appears is that in contrast with the Christian conception of authority, and in the splitting away from it, political thought has moved either to the divinization of the state or to the secular form of democracy where authority is denigrated and laws are made void of any moral sanction.

In the secular state, and above all in the Communist state, there is only one power, but this one power usually has to meet uneasy tensions. The politicians, being libertarians, do not dream of persecuting religion. They would prefer to treat it as a purely private affair, an experience some may enjoy in their closet. As, however, the modern democratic state is as much the offspring of the Christian philosophy as of Rousseau and the French free thinkers, and as it contains within it bodies of Christians who cannot be ignored, its effort is to strike some kind of a bargain with them. The temporal power acknowledges the existence of a spiritual power and is anxious for a good neighbor policy. Outside the totalitarian state, therefore, Church and state, Christian bodies and national government, continue today as they have co-existed since the time of Constantine. Close friendship, concordats, bare tolerance, all kinds of relationships have been set up from the Anglican establishment in England to the neutrality of the United States. There are some Christian bodies which are almost content to be identified with the state, so long as they are left free to practice their religion. The Catholic Church, once again, is thought to need careful watching, because of its intransigence and its reputation for being oversensitive and at the same time meddlesome. The historians of Europe devote many pages to the quarrels between Churchmen and Kings, and these happened in the days when all were of one faith. Undoubtedly there has been a chronic tension between the representatives of the two powers, spiritual and temporal. This has been due in part to the clash of strong personalities, to the type of Guelph and Ghibelline quarrels when the Popes ruled over the Papal States, but the principal cause lies in this that it is one and the same individual who has civil and religious ties. How, it is asked, can an individual have two loyalties and be faithful to both? The answer to this question brings us back to the declared opposition between Christianity and communism and their contrasting views of society and the destiny of human life.

The Communist argues that religion is a lie which acts as a drag on the progress of human society and says furthermore that Catholics, for example, are bound to be disloyal citizens in a Communist state. They are forbidden to believe in it. On the principle that one cannot serve both God and mammon, this latter accusation is true. In the Catholic view atheistic materialism is a form of government which is actively hostile to the essential interests of man, and therefore, so far as it puts theory into practice, it would be a betrayal of God to support it actively. This extreme case serves as an illustration of the attitude of the Church to society. This attitude was formulated as early as the fifth century in a letter of the Pope Gelasius to the Emperor Anastasius and repeated down the centuries. One such recent declaration is to the effect that "the limits of rights and duties once and for all defined (between the two powers), it is abundantly clear that rulers of States are free to administer their own affairs and that not only with the passive toleration of the Church but plainly with her active co-operation. . . . Church and State have each its own province in which each is supreme; therefore neither owes obedience to the other in the administration of its own affairs within the boundaries appointed to each." This looks straightforward, but in fact the perfect separation and at the same time co-operation have proved difficult to arrange. Quite apart from the totalitarian demands of dictators the growth of uniformity and state control in most modern states has led to what the Church regards as unwarrantable interference with its rights. The Church is allowed to worship, to teach religion privately and to administer the sacraments; these are obviously outside the competence of the lay authority. But the individual, who is left free to go to worship, is also a social being and falls under the social legislation of the state and has to follow its educational program. This legislation may in the eyes of the Church be immoral and the education may become so lay and antireligious as to undo the work of the Church. Hence the spiritual power insists that "if the Church considers it improper to meddle without reason with the government in worldly affairs and purely political matters, she is within her rights in seeking to prevent the civil power making that an excuse to oppose in any way whatsoever the superior interests which involve man's eternal salvation, to endanger or injure those interests by unjust laws or commands, to attack the divine constitution of the Church, or tread underfoot the sacred rights of God in the civil society of men."

This is not to claim rivalry with the civil power, nor does it amount to two allegiances. "There are not," as Suarez said, "two powers in the Supreme Pontiff, but one only relating directly to spiritual things and by way of consequence to temporal things."

Such "temporal things" refer above all to morals, and to show how actual this claim of the Church is, we have only to think of examples close at hand in time or space. A Christian, if asked to take part in the incineration of Jews, would be bound to refuse, and he could not be excused on the plea that the state had ordered him to take part. Delicate questions arose also during the war about the right to bomb non-combatant villages or towns. In hospitals it is always possible that a secular government may advocate operations or euthanasia which are repugnant to the Christian conscience. Such instances, and they can be multiplied, show how the spiritual power and the temporal power may be in opposition, and why it is that the Church claims to have the right to interfere on specific issues with the temporal power. Such interferences, however, annoy both the governments which have come to regard themselves as the ultimate court of appeal on all questions, and also the individual who has lost the sense of authority. Authority is looked upon as an interference with his liberty, and as nothing else. Without realizing it he has adopted an idea of liberty which is independent of any order or end and gives credit to any act so long as it is free. Such a belief digs its own grave, for, as we have seen, authority when it is unrecognized in its proper guise comes back in the shape of a tyranny. From what has been said about Catholic authority it is plain that it cannot be equated with that of the Kremlin or Fascist and Nazi despotism. The story of human frailty, of the abuse of power and of lamentable incidents, has to be read in the context of an ideal which puts in the first place human responsibility and human freedom, and invokes the direst penalties on those who, called to office in order to serve, lay unfair burdens on others and rule harshly and for their own ends. That fanaticism which so often distorts true zeal is counteracted by the demand for charity and reasonableness. Indeed many groups of Christians complain that the Catholic fondles reason too much when he should be leaning on pure faith. What is asked of him is a reasonable and intelligent obedience, one which is free, complete and loving, and not unlike what the great Bracton expected of an English citizen who was *liber et legalis homo*.

In the Christian theory of the two powers we have seen that each has its own domain, but the spiritual power has the right to interfere with the temporal when the latter commits wrong against its citizens. This demarcation might be taken to imply that the Christian *qua* Christian has no direct interest in human society. That this is not so is proved by the enormous influence which the Church has had on the formation of the societies of the West. Where the Christian philosophy is operative and dominant it is bound to show itself in the attitude of the state to human life, to liberty, and to the principles of justice. It, so to speak, animates the whole body. But while this is true it does not completely answer the question as to the relation which Christianity has to a human society and how far it is committed to helping it. What, in other words, is the full answer to the gibe of the Communist that the Christian religion is essentially otherworldly and not interested in the social affairs of man? The answer is not unanimous. Dr. H. Richard Niebuhr in a book, *Christ and Culture,* has tried to classify the varying answers under three headings. The first he calls the dualist position, which he holds was represented by such different persons as St. Paul, Tertullian, Luther, and Tolstoy. If, as he says, we define culture as "that total process of human activity and that total result of such activity to which now the name culture, now the name civilization, is applied in common speech," then those whom he has named would regard any compromise with it as impossible. Such a cultural society is "the world" with which Christ would have no dealings. In this view original sin meant universal corruption, not only, that is, the weakness which makes sin easy, but the total inability to act righteously. With such a "world" the Christian has nothing in common; it cannot be put right and contact with it may bring contamination. Hence the Christian must aim at separation from it and fasten his mind on what is holy and incorruptible, the everlasting way of life revealed by God. The perfection he must seek is, in Niebuhr's words, "wholly distinct from the aims men seek in politics and economics, in science and arts."

The second position is that of a liaison or compromise. There are two demands made upon the Christian, which are at first sight incompatible; his task is nevertheless to make a synthesis of them and to use as a motto "Both Christ and culture." On the one hand is the commandment to sell everything for the sake of following him, to give up judging our fellows, to turn the other cheek to the violent, to humble ourselves and become the servants of all, to abandon family, and to forget tomorrow. On the other hand, the Christian is born into a family and into a community; he has his daily duties and multitudinous cares, his talents and his affections. This world is also the creation of God and cannot be separated by a wave of the hand from the supernatural vocation revealed to him in Christ. The commandments to be observed in daily life are challenges to his free will and just as much divine precepts as those of the Sermon on the Mount. Niebuhr cites St. Thomas Aquinas as the protagonist of this view that a reconciliation must be sought between the two pressures on conscience, for "man's search for unity is unconquerable, and the Christian has a special reason for seeking integrity because of his fundamental faith in the God who is One."

The third position Niebuhr calls "conversionist." Amongst its advocates he enumerates the Gnostics, Abelard, St. Augustine, and in modern times Ritschl and F. D. Maurice. They all agree in holding that the ideal of a Christian society can be realized in this world. The "dear city of Cecrops" can become the city of Zeus, and the "hard sayings" of Christ can be lived in an earthly society. Ritschl is quoted: "The Christian idea of the kingdom of God denotes the association of mankind—an association both extensively and intensively the most comprehensible possible—through the reciprocal moral action of its members, action which transcends all merely natural and particular associations," and if this is not very clear some help to understanding may be given by Niebuhr's remark that "the conversion of mankind from self-centeredness to Christ-centeredness was for Maurice the universal and present divine possibility."

Christians do certainly blow hot or cold on the possibility of forming a truly Christian society, and they are also at variance on the question whether such a supposed society is to be equated with the Kingdom of God preached by Christ. The divisions, however, given by Niebuhr are a little sketchy and suffer through a neglect of the presuppositions of the writers he mentions. Passages from St. Paul, for instance, could be quoted in favor of all three positions. It is extraordinary to find the Gnostics amongst the advocates of a perfect, Christian earthly society; they hated the body and carried to an extreme the Platonic devaluation of the fleeting image of this world. Without knowing the presuppositions of the Christians mentioned we are sure to be led astray. Tertullian, for instance, ended as a Montanist heretic and the Gnostics were regarded by the great Christian thinkers as enemies of human nature. What makes Christians differ is due partly to their understanding of original sin and partly to their conception of the Church. Luther and many who followed him held that original sin brought universal corruption. It follows obviously that grace and nature have nothing in common, and that no good can be expected from human society. In Luther's view the state is a consequence of original sin and to be endured no matter how evil. It is man's punishment. As he says: "The Proverbs, which talk about mercy belong to the Kingdom of God and to the Christians but not the earthly Kingdom—The secular Kingdom is nothing but the servant of God's ire towards the wicked, and a fore-taste of hell and eternal death." Not all accepted this consequence; indeed in the nineteenth century among liberal Christians the idea was dropped, and instead, men like Maurice fought for a Christian Socialism. The pendulum swung again back to Luther and Calvin in the twentieth century, and Karl Barth has been bearing witness to the absolute gulf between the word of God and any human language or merit or ideal. Human history is for him a waste product. The Christian Socialists, however, have revived the idea of a perfect Christian society, for, as we have seen, Dr. Paul Tillich minimizes the distinction between the supernatural and the natural, the Christian ideal and the ideal of society. "Church and society are one in their essential nature; for the substance of culture is religion and the form of religion is culture."

The Catholic doctrine of original sin differs from that of Luther and Calvin, and consequently, as might be expected, the first position as described by Niebuhr is not a Catholic one. Human nature was not totally corrupted by original sin. The essence of that sin lies in the loss of God's friendship which had been cemented by the gift of supernatural union. This supernatural union was lost, and without it the integrity of human nature has been so weakened that there is a bias to the lesser good and to evil. But as human nature is not evil, there is no reason for making the complete separation of the Christian and human ideal. Where the Catholic thinkers split into two schools is in their estimate of the degree or weight of this bias. In its practical attitude the Church has swayed from one side to the other according to the experience it has had of contact with society. At first it was so horrified with the viciousness of ancient Rome that it intended to keep away from the world. Then when the Empire began to fall to pieces and the welfare of society almost depended upon the action of the Church it became the cultural commissariat of Western society and deeply involved in its activities. The multiple commitments lowered the standards of Christians, clerical and lay, and a cry went up against this laxity and worldliness. The result was a new outburst of unworldly advice and practice, so marked in the spirit of St. Francis of Assisi and in the rules of the new order which he founded. The same see-saw continued. By the sixteenth century corruption was rampant in the very center of Christendom, and once more the note of total abstention from the world was sounded. What St. Francis was to the thirteenth century, the mystical reaction of St. Teresa and St. John of the Cross was to the post-Reformation period. This swinging from one side to the other has its parallel in the theological field. Niebuhr quotes St. Thomas Aquinas as a synthetist. What he says is true, but not all were in agreement with St. Thomas. What is called the Augustinian school, both in its theology and in its spiritual teaching leant more to the side of unworldliness, the having as little as possible to do with the world. St. Augustine, *pace* Dr. Niebuhr, had hard words to say on merely human virtues. St. Francis wanted no book learning in his order and treated his body as a Brother Ass—mule might have been the better name. The high point of this attitude is to be found in that classic which even "the George Eliots" treasured, *The Imitation of Christ,* by Thomas à Kempis.

What is evident both from the practice and theory of the Catholic Church is that the supernatural and the natural are inevitably partners, but uneasy partners. The texts which Niebuhr quoted, especially from the Sermon on the Mount, point the way to perfection as Christianity understands it. Unless a man puts God first and so much first that everything else, family, friends, and human society and life itself, is by comparison as nothing, he cannot begin to enter into the mystery of Christian love and perfection. But these texts, which are at first sight so forbidding and uncompromising, have to be read in the light of other texts and of the whole scheme of life taught by Christ. They presuppose the goodness of nature and of human persons and human associations. They are like the hillside which is very steep and which must be climbed before we can see from the top the world with a better sight and with a truer appreciation. This is the world which has to be restored to truth, and not ignored or passed by. In it alone can human character be developed and the mind come to a realization of itself and of the worth of others. The individual who has a light is not supposed to hide it under a bushel, or his talents under a cloth.

The problem for the Christian, therefore, is not one of complete denial, but of the degree of his mixing with the world and society. The Churchman, whose vocation by its very nature is to be occupied with the forms of divine worship and the spiritual interests of his neighbor, should exhibit above all the unworldly aspect of the Christian life. The layman, on the other hand, with family and society obligations and the day-in day-out cares and joys of labor and profession, has the more complicated problem of aiming at perfection in and through his secular activities. So complicated and difficult is this task that there is a widespread notion that the Church, like some eastern religions, has two grades, the one of perfection reserved for monks and nuns and the clergy and the other for the layman. The layman is not expected to fulfill the ideals of the Gospel. The pegs for the high jump are deliberately lowered. This is an error, though one easy to commit. No one is absolved from seeking for perfection, and all are given grace to reach it. But at the same time the Christian in society has, as it were, to live two lives, to have two intentions, and to strive to make them one. He has to make a success of his work, to advance in his profession, to love what is worth loving around him and not let it get in the way of the supreme love. He has to seek the temporal good of the group and country to which he belongs, to pursue the work he is doing without distraction and wholeheartedly, and yet not make an idol of it or become so absorbed as to forget "the one thing necessary." The apparent dichotomy can be overcome, but it is idle to think that this is a child's game. In *Grey Eminence* Aldous Huxley depicts the self-deception of a man of God who mixes his religion with the mundane service of his country. This is failure on a high level because Huxley makes it clear that Père Joseph was a man of great austerity, given to fasting and prayer. What is far more frequent is the quick or slow acceptance of the standards of life around one. Christianity knows from experience that one can sup with the devil only with a long spoon. In every century preachers and poets have declaimed against the worldliness of the clergy and of the Christians in high positions. Even the good take on the character of their surroundings, as the recent case of the Worker Priests in France proves. The influence of the herd on the individual is very strong, as also that of the trade and the business and the climate of the age. This is good Communist doctrine, up to a point. The bourgeois and the worker are conditioned to think differently, but the individual is not so cabined and confined as the Communist thinks. He is always free and he is always in danger, and this is the theme of innumerable novels, the Troilus and Cressida refrain, the fate of Angelo, Major Barbara, and Scobie.

There is always, therefore, a tension, a struggle within and without in the Christian life. He looks within and meets lethargy, self-indulgence, and a divided self, and he confronts a world outside which is as much a tempter as an ally. The climate of society is constantly varying. Hopkins saw a world charged with the grandeur of God, but scared with trade and wearing man's smudge. To Eliot it is "the land of lobelias and tennis flannels . . . and the wind shall say: 'Here were decent godless people: Their only monument the asphalt road and a thousand lost golf balls!' " Present-day society has very little likeness to the sharply defined one which Marx drew with his laws of production at his elbow. So much of man was left out, and science has made such discoveries that his picture is all askew. No threat of hydrogen bombs and man-killing radioactivity disturbed his dreams of the classless society. Nor did he realize how dependent man is for his daily joys on the ever-increasing delicacy of his nervous organism, and the recurrence of bad dreams and the boredom of material prosperity and the jealousies aroused by the promises of better days and equality for everyone. It is possible for a society to be so darkened to truth as Christians understand it that in the words of the gospel the preachers of it must wipe the dust off their feet and depart; or it may be so agog with excitement at news of some fresh promised land that it has not time to listen to Christian philosophy—and there is always the danger of Christian truth being twisted or cut to the pattern of the fashionable ideas of the time.

For these and many other reasons the relations between Christianity and human society cannot be formulated and predicted in the semi-scientific manner which Marxism has adopted. Anyone is free to take up a hopeful or pessimistic view of what the future has in store. There are, it is true, hints and even promises in the New Testament, but there is no sure interpretation of what they mean, so far as life on earth is concerned. The pessimists quote the words about the absence of faith which Christ is to find when he returns. The more hopeful, and those who represent a new school of Christian theology, emphasize the texts which tell us of a new heaven and a new earth. The appearance of this latter and apocalyptic view seems to be episodic. Its most famous exponent was the Abbot Joachim of Flora, who lived in the latter half of the twelfth century. His views were received with great acclaim and he is celebrated by Dante as "Calabria's Abbot Joachim endowed with soul prophetic." A faithful adherent of the Church, he, nevertheless, foresaw, claiming that he had

had a private revelation on the point, a time when the age of faith would be succeeded by an age of love. The Old Testament was the age of the Father, that of the New Testament the Age of the Son, and the final Age would be that of the Holy Spirit, who is "to lead us into all truth." In the first of these times man lived in fear and under the Law; in the second, man lived under the new Covenant and by faith. The third period is of the kingdom which will be ruled by love—"they will burn with love," and this kingdom is to be realized upon the earth.

If we are allowed to imagine the classless society to be one in which men and women are moved by love more than by the economic necessities of production, the visions of Marx and Joachim become not too unlike. But to many both Marx and Joachim are daydreaming; they ignore the cloud which is creeping up the sky, the cloud for which real scientists are responsible and not the science which fills the pages of Marx. The thought behind men's minds is that there is no future. In all past predicaments the worst conceivable was only a partial destruction or collapse, and human means could be thought of which could avert it. For the first time a monstrous weapon has been discovered which is not partial in its effects nor can it be managed in the way past scientific discoveries could be turned to good. As an American writer has put it: "There is no reasonable or 'liberal' way to drop a hydrogen bomb on a city. It makes no difference who administers a war of total annihilation. In such a struggle, there is no lesser evil of one side against the other. There is only the monstrous common evil." He then goes on to quote a saying that the third world war will not be a fight of Russians against Americans but of Russians and Americans against the common enemy, humanity. If this be so then we are facing a situation which has no alternatives; there is no longer any solution within history. The secular hope comes to an end, and neither the rationalist nor the positive historian has anything to say. Only the religious mind can find an alternative and a hope by relying on a God who is above history.

The logical conclusion from this is that the ultimate hope of society cannot be placed in any one political or national power, not even in a supra-national group of powers so long as the world remains divided as it is. Is then the choice that between the yogi and the commissar? Not the commissar, because he is dedicated to the destruction of the capitalist nations. The yogi would welcome peace, but he has not in mind to do anything to promote it. He seeks for a state of mind where all the tumults of the world die away and he is absorbed into the quiet of another world. This is a form of escape which has distinguished propagandists. The Christian rejects it because it is a form of escape, and he is committed to this world where God became incarnate. He combines faith in God and faith in human society, and this, maybe, is the greatest contribution he can make in the present crisis. And the reason for saying this can be found in the words of Cardinal Schuster, apropos of the political efforts being made by the West to form a common front. "It is a poor Bishop, in the see of St. Ambrose, who meditates and weeps over present political conditions. When, in order to halt the barbarian invaders on the Alpine route, the declining

Empire found nothing better to do than to block the passes with barricades, the Bishop of Milan invented a name for this kind of defense: *vallum pudoris* [rampart of shame]. I do not dare to say the same thing of the various present-day projects for various degrees of 'Europeanism,' but I feel, all the same, that the common Christian conscience, beneath the political combination, must once again constitute the most efficacious defense of humanity."

A gentle skepticism about some of the means concerted by nations and international bodies for insuring future peace can go along with readiness to assist in every way possible. Assistance is not a courtesy but a duty; the Christian is not breaking his journey out of benevolence like the Samaritan to pick up the wounded. They belong to the same army and are engaged on the same campaign. They are both members of a human society, and each in his own way is in duty bound to serve its interests. Differences can arise about what makes human society work and work to the ultimate good of the individuals composing it, and indeed, as in the case of communism in Russia, they can reach to utter discrepancy. Usually, as in the liberal or neutral states, a *modus vivendi* can be reached and concordats drawn up because there is much in common, belief in the individual, in liberty of association, of education, of family life, and a general maintenance of the moral order. An individual can work within the constitution for the changes he may think necessary and for the bettering of human relations. The basic Christian belief is that progress in society can be made only by a firm and deep understanding of the nature of society, and its dependence on natural law, and that even this is not enough. As city dwellers must take a holiday by the sea or in the hills, human society needs the air of the religious ideal to keep it from falling sick. The lovely image of Plato of the fish in the sea of Salamis which leap above the waters to greet the rising sun is applicable to the city of man. "When a man loses the idea of God he loses the true knowledge of himself," for he is "the fountain light of all our day" and "master light of all our seeing." For the truth of this in practice we have the comment of a historian on the work of the Saxon missionaries in Germany that "their creative civilizing power in this world arose precisely from the fact that they had their gaze fixed on the next."

On this basis Christian sociologists have prepared a program which, if too philosophic to be to the taste of modern positivists, nevertheless comes down to earth in its proposals for the distribution of property and the giving of a just wage. Worked out in a period of capitalist competition it is greatly concerned that justice be done to the workers and that the opportunities of a full life should be opened out to them. Such a social ethic is meant not only to safeguard justice, the foundation of any society, but also to give positive aid in bringing about concord between nations and a lasting peace. Within the moral principles set forth there is plenty of room for difference of political and social views. A society is not bound to any one kind of government. No government can rule without the implicit or explicit consent of the governed, and its general aim must be such as to promote the good of the people. But people vary in their degree of development, and what is suitable for a backward and growing nation may not be enlightened enough for a full-grown civilization. Nor is a Christian obliged to extol the people's voice as the voice of God; neither historically nor theoretically can such a claim be made out. Socialism, in so far as it proclaims as a dogma that the state should and must take over all the means of production, is regarded by Catholic moralists as a definite threat to the rights of the individual. The state should act on the long range ideal of redistributing property so that the individual is capable of enjoying it and using it to the general interest. In a sense quite different from that of the classless society of Marx the interference of the state should diminish the more the members of it grow in wisdom and in fellowship. In the meantime, however, the state is justified in nationalizing industries when it is convinced that the long-range aim is thereby brought nearer.

In its interpretation, too, of liberty the Catholic moralist strikes a mean between the Communist and the individualistic view. The theory of Rousseau set no limits to the liberty of the individual. That man had behaved badly in the past was attributed to the limitations imposed upon him by irrational laws and regulations. Once man had shaken off his chains his nature would grow unimpededly, and freedom and happiness would become in time synonymous. The nineteenth century put this theory to the test, above all in the sphere of economics. Unrestricted competition was defended, no matter what suffering it brought, on the ground that it was bound to lead to the greatest happiness of the greatest number. But so flagrantly false did this finally prove to be that in the outcry against the inequalities in wealth, the formation of companies and trusts and cartels, public opinion swung over to the opposite of this unbridled competition. So incapable had the individual shown himself of using his liberty fairly and of disposing of his property and possessions to the common good that a theory rapidly gained ground which in fact took this liberty away. Since, that is, the individual could not be trusted with ownership all ownership should be handed over to the state. Only the state is in a position to look after the welfare of the people. The general will of the people as incorporated in a government, replaced, as a consequence, the conscience of the individual. The Catholic view lies between these two, in that it neither despairs of the individual nor puts entire faith in his angelic disposition. A schooling is required even more for the character than for the mind, if the divided will is to be cured and the habits of virtue formed. It is somewhat strange that a double process should be going on at the same time, the emphasis on liberty almost to the exclusion of other human values and the withdrawal of it from the individual into the hands of the state. If the ownership of property has been abused, the answer consistently should be not deprivation but training in responsibility and in the right meaning of liberty. That political minds have lagged behind and not seen the connection between liberty and the need of discipline in its right use is shown in the growing complaint that science, in discovering and developing new engines of power, has run ahead of the moral capacity of man to control them. In his presidential address to the British Association in 1954 Dr. Adrian warned his audience of the dangers not only of the atom bomb but also of the radioactivity generated by it, and added: "Our behavior must be made worthy of our increased knowledge." This could be done, he suggested, by more science, by the study of behavior in the individual and in the mass. What needs greater recognition is that the problem is a moral one, and consists in the proper use of our liberty, which cannot be secured save by the love and understanding of a moral and religious ideal and by the hard way of discipline in good habits. What is more to the point, there can be no promise of a fully human and happy society on earth unless the individuals who compose society combine service to the community with a full life of independence. The well-known remark of Edmund Burke is applicable here, that "society cannot exist unless a controlling power upon will and appetite be placed somewhere, and the less of it there is within, the more there must be without. It is ordained in the eternal constitution of things, that men of intemperate minds cannot be free." The controlling power in the Soviet Union has not shown any signs of passing to the people and of their being trained to use it rightly; it is exercised more and more from without, and this is one of the reasons why men like Gide and Silone decided that salvation could not come out of Russia. Nor can it be found by any scientific treatment of man. Ways may be found of conditioning him, of making him less mad by leucotomy and more amenable by other kinds of operation or feeding or psychical manipulation; but a sub-human society will be the only result. The kingdom of God is within, and there is no means of by-passing the only way of human development, which is by freedom and self-determination, aided by grace.

The main Christian tradition, therefore, and, as it must be allowed, the only view inclusive of the multi-colored pattern of Christianity is that which Niebuhr called the synthetic. Léon Bloy called himself a "pilgrim of the absolute." Human beings are pilgrims of eternity in time and their eternity depends upon their use of time and their love of their fellow men; they have to labor in the hope that "your young men shall see visions and your old men dream dreams." The Christian equally with the Marxist has a passion for the redemption of his fellow men—and, what is more, he is confident that he has in his religion the wherewithal to bring it about. As Professor Arnold Toynbee has said: the world cannot be written off as a failure, for God does not make unsuccessful experiments. Still less can it be regarded as "a realm of Chaos and Ancient Night altogether outside God's jurisdiction." It must be a precious part of God's realm, because God so loved it as to become a member of it, to die for it and rise again to be its new Head. This, to repeat, is the source of the Christian belief in human society, and in the Christian philosophy, in its combination of the highest wisdom of man and the knowledge of God's intentions for man, can be found an efficacious program for building up individual character, social good will and international peace.

8. Conclusion

So serious, however, is the present crisis of civilization and so pressing is the demand for an alternative to the Communist solution that many Christians are searching for a fresh and closer co-operation of Christianity with human society. I have already mentioned some of the expedients suggested by modern Christian thinkers to meet the crisis. Some favor collaboration with the Marxist social philosophy; others demand cordial relations and a truce on criticism. Others again would reinterpret relevant texts of Scripture and argue that the kingdom of heaven of the Gospels is meant to be fulfilled in a human society on earth. Professor D. M.

Mackinnon bravely urges that the death of Christ the Godman upon a cross and his resurrection give the clue to the only dialectic which offers universal hope.

This, indeed, is the kernel of Christian belief, and it re-echoes the cry of St. Paul, that "we preach Christ and him crucified." But while this must be done, there are other things which must not be left undone. It is right, for instance, to expose the truth or falsehood of communism, to estimate its truth and weakness, and to set alongside it the Christian doctrine of man and of society. There is the more need of this as both sides are racing against each other, and both proclaim a universal faith, a philosophy of life, and set a high value on action. The Communist seems to have an advantage in that his news is comparatively fresh, while Christianity looks to many so wrinkled with age and its language has lost its bite. Communism, too, is one's neighbor at home and in the factory and field, while Christianity, it is thought, is found in a church or chapel; and lastly communism claims to bring a remedy here and now to our material needs, our physical hunger and our physical poverty as well as for our thirst for justice; while Christianity, we are told, bids us put up with the ills of this life for a reward in a kingdom to come. The religion of the Cross is also the religion of the resurrection, and the present world would be glad to know whether this doctrine of the resurrection flows over to water also the dry lands which the Communist promises to irrigate.

The answer is in the affirmative, and the past history of the West, and to some extent of the East as well, bears witness to the efforts to promote man's well-being. Time and history do play a part in the Christian religion which marks it off from all others, and in some mysterious way time is redeemed and the human actions of man are not lost once they are performed. It would take us too far from the subject to explain how this is possible. If we sow in history we reap in eternity, and the Christian belief contains both. Nothing is gained by denying or minimizing "the immortality of the soul beyond the grave." In truth the completion of "all things in Christ" remains mysterious, and it is dangerous to apply it too literally to ideas of historical progress or to any form of social or political change in society. Such speculation can be left to the philosopher of history or to the Marxist, though in justice to the Marxist he can in his best moments be acquitted of mere theory. His emphasis is on action, and the Christian meets him at that point. Each individual has his Sparta and his task is to be a credit to it and to make it better. He mingles in the life of his town and country. He may have a family to provide for and a house to look after; he goes to his shop or factory or office and has a concrete piece of work to do. All this he shares with those of other beliefs and varying ages; and the only difference between him and other citizens is the interior motive which activates him. In the New Testament Christ is declared to be the new Lord of life, to whom all things have been made subject. This is the faith: "The earth is the Lord's and the fulness thereof; the Lord reigns as king, and his name shall be peerless, God prince of peace, father of eternity, and of his kingdom there shall be no end." With such a belief a Christian cannot be a disinterested spectator of what happens in the world around him or just lend a hand in business which is not his direct concern. In and through the demands made upon him by his country, the government and his chiefs, he reads the authority of Him who has taken over the government of the world, and this is the secret of his obedience and why in the letters of St. Paul the early Christians are told to obey their temporal masters. His first aim is justice, the promotion of right relations between the members of the society in which he lives, and secondly a love which is self-forgetful.

While, therefore, there is no certain promise of a perfectly ordered society coming true, and the Christian is more realistic in this than the Marxist, the unstinted devotion to justice and charity is the one sure means of making life in this world as nearly happy as it can be. One is free to believe that with the growing knowledge of technology and the ever-increasing attention to the problems of poverty, of health, of housing, of the proper distribution of wealth, of the better understanding of the inter-relation of body and mind, of the processes of habit formation and the good and bad effects of discipline, many of the sources of unhappiness, of envy and criminal tendencies can be removed. There is nothing in Christian belief which forbids the research into human problems of behavior or the right application of scientific discovery. So far from this being so, a Christian is bound to believe in the God-given powers of the mind and will. Where alone he will hesitate is in the use and application of knowledge; we are as tempted today as in the past to be penny wise and pound foolish and through sentiment or partisanship and hasty judgment to put second things first. The enormous improvements which have been made in civilization, in the "decencies" of life, the care for the weak and old, the education of the people, the unprejudiced administration of justice, are a fair augury of the future. Persons can pass from one country to another without molestation, and within most countries the old harshnesses and brutalities have been practically abolished.

The return, however, of barbarism whenever the traditional patterns of behavior are disturbed does not allow us to indulge in utopian dreams. Hence there will be amongst Christians as amongst all groups the optimists and the conservatives who will interpret their experience of human nature differently. "You can expel nature with a fork, but it will always come back," and original sin, unlike cancer, is universal and a part of our make-up. The optimists with reason take a long view and compare the condition of primitive peoples with civilization today. If, they argue, such an undoubted advance has been made, what is there to prevent a similar advance in the future? Moreover those who believe in God are warranted in thinking that the very gradualness in the development of knowledge, of physical nature and of the human body corroborates a belief in the further perfecting of human nature. Human knowledge is not to be considered as something separate from man himself; it is an outstanding characteristic of man, and where such an important part of him grows the rest should also grow, otherwise man would become lopsided, and such a phenomenon would reflect on the providence of God, unless, that is, the lopsidedness were man's own fault. That man may, indeed, be at fault is suggested by what many of the scientists are now feeling. Their conscience is pricked at the vast new powers they are handing over to governments and peoples at a time when they can be so abused. As they say the moral ideal has not kept abreast of the pursuit of scientific knowledge. But such a temporary failing would not clash with the hope that in the long run a society may use the constantly growing knowledge to its benefit, as in the past; despite many failures and defeats, man has progressed.

Communism and Christianity have, therefore, both of them the interest of society and of the world at heart, and they stand over against one another pledged to different means and to different ideals. They have been called rival religions, but this is to abuse words, and it is better to speak of rival faiths. A faith can be described as a theory of life, held passionately as an ideal which can be attained by action. Both the two rivals have such a faith, though the Christian holds that only by grace can the ideal be reached. There have been many faiths which now slumber or are dead. In the middle of the nineteenth century many thought that Christianity was becoming effete. Now, however, if we may take the well-informed weekly, *Time*, for witness: "Every week, in pulpits, editorials, Parliaments and Chanceries, in universities, clinics, and at cocktail parties, Christianity is invoked. Juvenile delinquency? Broken homes? Neuroses? 'The answer is a sound Christian upbringing.' High divorce rate? Alcoholism? Disintegrating ethics? 'We need a firm Christian morality.' Is science getting out of hand? Are art and literature aimless? 'Christianity gives the only aim.' Communism? 'Only Christianity can defeat a false religion.' A more complex highbrow version of the mood is expressed by British historian Arnold Toynbee, who concludes his massive, ten-volume *A Study of History* with the finding that the West can be saved from atomic war and utter downfall only by a renewed Christian faith."

But what is it in communism that makes it so alive today and successful in gaining converts? Some would answer that it is the lay version of Christian hope with all the superstitious and supernatural trimmings of the Christian religion left out. Analyzing the motives of six distinguished writers who had for a time turned Communist, Mr. Crossman in *The God That Failed* says that they saw communism as "a vision of the Kingdom of God on earth; and like Wordsworth and Shelley, they dedicated their talents to working humbly for its coming." There were many others, who in the period between the October Revolution and the Stalin-Hitler Pact were attracted to the same faith. "They had a heightened perception of the spirit of the age, and felt more acutely than others both its frustrations and its hopes." They "had a premonition of catastrophe, they looked for a philosophy with which they could analyse it and overcome it—and many of them found what they needed in Marxism." The choice in those years was between two materialistic philosophies; one that of capitalism, which relied on automatic Progress, and made so-called democracy a weapon to crush human freedom, and "a Left which seemed eager to use it in order to free humanity." With such alternatives it is no wonder that so many embraced the Communist cause. Whittaker Chambers in his *Witness* reviewing his own motives for joining communism is at pains to make clear from his own experience and that of others what it is that makes communism so attractive. It must make some profound appeal to the human mind. It is absurd, he says, to think of it as "a vicious plot hatched by wicked men in a sub-cellar." He agrees with Crossman in thinking that the intellectual is inspired by a vision; but the working man is "chiefly moved by the crisis"; and it is a fact that communism has received its largest number of converts at moments of crisis such as the rise of fascism, the American economic crash and the Spanish civil war. Men and women in such crises turn to find some solution, and the Communist faith was able to make a unique appeal. First it dealt in black or white, a simple alternative which makes loyalty and understanding so easy and final. Then what it has to say came pat on the crisis; it seemed to be the obvious cap which fitted the need. But more than this: it offered a faith which called for all the latent powers of depressed men and women, and gave an individual importance in the movement, a function to each and every one. "Philosophers have explained the world; it is necessary to change it." These ringing words of Marx summoned men to act and to successful acts. The onus of changing the world to the heart's delight was no longer in God's hands or that of mysterious powers or governments. For the first time man could do without these mythical or false aids and accomplish what he had formerly prayed God to do. The chaos of life will be reduced to order; science is on the side of

Marxism; it is unquestionably right. Hence communism in the view of Chambers is "the vision of man's mind displacing God as the creative intelligence of the world. It is the vision of man's liberated mind, by the sole force of its rational intelligence, redirecting man's destiny and reorganizing man's life and the world."

Chambers quotes a remark made to him by Krivitsky: "Looked at concretely, there are no ex-communists. There are only revolutionists and counter-revolutionists." The point of this remark is that the world is going through a supreme crisis; that the Communists are revolutionaries who are changing it to their ideals, and that to counter them the other side must be equally revolutionary if it is to have any chance of succeeding. There is a touch of mob oratory in such a remark, the while it has a truth which the Christian should be the first to recognize. He knows too well that in times past Churches in various countries have been too subservient and ready to serve two masters. The number of nominal Christians, who fail to put into practice what they are supposed to believe, is vast. The frightening truths of the Gospels have been muted or twisted out of recognition, and many have been contented with a formal Sunday observance. If by revolutionary is meant the putting into practice of the precepts and counsels of Christianity, then indeed the Communist faith cannot be met except by a faith which is held as strongly and put into action. There are, however, innumerable persons who do with a quiet mind and without fanaticism or emotional violence live the Christian life. They are unnoticed and not taken into account because they do not imitate the methods of infiltration and propaganda employed by the Communists. The two sides rely on utterly different motives and resources. The Communist thinks of nothing but the new and perfect society, whose plans are already laid, and he is confident that this is all there is to think about, and that the resources he can rely on are sufficient. The Christian does not wager all on this earthly society; he does not believe that man will ever find his complete satisfaction there. In these desperate times he is called upon as if the one purpose of Christianity was to doctor human society, as a Michelangelo might be called in to correct the bad drawing of pupils. But it cannot be too often repeated that Christianity was not founded to lead any nation or super-nation to prosperity. This was the mistake of the Jews, and when the people sought to make Christ king, he fled away from them into the mountain. God, the object of religion, cannot be appropriated by any nation or any time; he transcends earthly societies and has to be worshiped "in spirit and in truth." Those who have tasted of the "things of the spirit," whether in the East or the West, can never possibly find their portion on this earth. That is not to say that the Christian is uninterested. What he does now is of vital importance to him, and there is an intimate connection between now and what is to come. Moreover he discovers that only by looking up and beyond the resources which he and his other fellow men have, can human affairs be kept from staggering into the ditch. He holds that life cannot be lived fully on its own terms; if it is to be safely human it must be grounded in something, which Bertrand Russell calls "in some sense outside of human life . . . above mankind." This fixed conviction can be seen in all the literature of Christendom, and is radiantly expressed by William Langland in *Piers Plowman*. "From the ragged root by Christian charity springs the rose that is red and sweet; For we are all Christ's creatures—and of his coffers rich, And brethren as of one blood—as well beggars as earls, For on Calvary of Christ's blood —Christendom gan spring, And blood brethren we became there—of one body won, As quasimodo geniti —and gentlemen each one. No beggar or serving boy among us—save sin made him so."

God and the worship of him to the Communist are a form of treachery to man. Religion is either a childish superstition or a myth invented in unscientific days to comfort the oppressed proletariat. Marx, it is thought, has settled the claims once and for all, and what gives urgency and passion to the Communist is the assurance that in his own hands for the first time is the remedy for human troubles. The Communists are the chosen people with the power to lead the nations into the promised land. The day is over when utopias and temporary ideologies should be presented to the people like mirages in the desert. Man is made from the earth and from the earth must come his salvation. All goes to show that a materialistic philosophy is right. It alone makes sense; it is scientific; it unites theory with action, and that action is the completion of what has been going on in history since man first became a productive animal by turning tools to use. Every change in history has been dictated by the productive forces which have followed a clearly seen dialectic. In that process the proletariat has moved from position to position, until now finally it is master of its fate. The people have come to the parting of the ways, and now they will have no dictators but themselves. They will do away with all opposition which has crushed or cramped them; they will have no need of governments; they will end wars, and in their union and unity will come to pass "the true resurrection of nature, the realized naturalism of men, the realized humanism of nature." Such a society will satisfy all the needs of man, all he can be or could wish to be. No heaven but a heavenly world.

The "classless society" is predestined, that is to say, it is scientifically certain, and therefore can be predicted. At the same time the Communist has to struggle might and main, as if the issue were uncertain and he had to fight to bring it about. The dialectic can be, and is, described by Marx in terms of economics, but his language is also of exhortation, a call to arms and to the dispersion of the enemy, the bourgeois capitalists. The bourgeois are excluded from the kingdom and all means of destroying them and their power are legitimate. Only now has a situation arisen in which the workers of the world have a full and proper say in economic production and in directing the forces of nature. They have come from nature, and they have been alienated from it, being forced to regard it as a force to be feared or as a system to which they were subject. Now nature and man are reconciled; man becomes fully natural and uses his liberty to understand and appreciate nature and to direct it in harmony with his own best interests. This reconciliation of man and nature, of freedom and necessity is what makes for full happiness. Even now in the interim before the end is attained there is no doubt that the member, locked in the embrace of the party and consumed with one idea, does have an almost cosmic sense of fulfilment and unity, and feels that nothing matters save fidelity to the cause and the beating down of all resistance to it.

While the Christian should be at least equally concerned with the welfare of his neighbor, he is bound to be in opposition to almost all the principles and points which unite the Communist. Even if the scientific pose of the Communist were more sound than it is, he would all the same deny that out of science human happiness can spring. Science produces the hydrogen bomb, and that bomb can put an end to all the hopes of a classless society emerging at the end of the dialectic of history. Marx lived too early to be able to see the monster which stands in the way of his neat dialectic; and if recourse be had to violence in the extermination of the "imperialists" then the Communist society will with the greatest probability also be exterminated. Neither violence nor dialectic have the last word here. The solution must be a moral or religious one, and there is far more need of putting into practice the Christian virtues than of mastering the Marxian system and technique. The Christian says that there is no mortal or necessary enmity between the classes, that those this side of the iron curtain as well as those beyond it are equally children of God, made in his image. The first object, therefore, in social and political programs must be not the exaltation of one group, large as it may be, but the unity of mankind in a lasting peace. Where so much power exists in the different nations of the world it must be harnessed to peaceful purposes, and this cannot be done unless the despised morality of Christianity be taken seriously and put into practice. When the Communists wish to rouse the people they appeal to this very morality; they use words which have kept the same meanings for hundreds of years. Justice and love of one's neighbor are not words invented by Barbarossa or the Stock Exchange; they are not the shibboleths of a class; they go back to the beginning of civilization; but they do not have their highest import until they are understood in the light of a God-made-man living and dying for mankind. This breath of the supernatural is, so the Christian believes, necessary to keep society alive to its obligations and ideals. There is no evidence whatsoever to prove that the productive forces of nature can produce human happiness; the curve of production touches it only intermittently, and where there is most material prosperity there there is tedium and rancor. The new psychology has revealed that the barbarian in us is not much affected by this world's goods, whether we have them or not.

> *Why should I not, had I the heart to do it,*
> *Like to the Egyptian thief at point of death,*
> *Kill what I love?*

What has been happening in Russia since the October Revolution has to be fitted into the Marxist predictions. We have seen Lenin's attempt to do this, and there have been many apologists for Stalin's policy and centralization of power. There have been also a number who have been so scandalized by the Stalin régime that they have fled Russia and denounced his betrayal of the Marxist ideal. The story of these years to an unbiased historian does confirm the Acton dictum of the corruption of power rather than the materialistic conception of history. It needs a strong faith to see in the liquidation of Lenin's friends, the changes of front which unfailingly gave more power to Stalin himself, the crushing of all exercise of freedom amongst the people, in this reappearance of an Eastern despotism, the growth of people's liberty and the rule of the proletariat. Acton's saying belongs to the Christian tradition. It is an admission of human fallibility joined to a belief in man when he co-operates with God. If we consult the great literature of the world and look at what it expresses of human aspiration, we shall find that much of it is outside the horizon of communism; the Bolshevist must condemn it as heresy or pernicious nonsense, fit only for burning. Only what is evil is excluded from the Christian philosophy, and within that philosophy the possibilities of evil as well as good are given full range. That is why the growth of centralization and autocracy cannot but be suspect to those who have been educated in the philosophy of the West. They have learnt to know what is in man, and so to guess what is most likely to happen when a clique is given power.

To the ideas, therefore, which are the very lifeblood of Communist action the Christian opposes a quite different set of ideas. The philosophies cannot be amalgamated, and the fundamental reason is that the one believes in God and the other leaves God out. The one starts from the bottom, the other from the top; halfway between is man. The one says that matter is the be-all and end-all. Out of that he has to construct the world we know, and explain the body, the mind and freedom of man, all that we know of man in history, his civilization, his science, his philosophy and art and religion, his errors and his vices, his friendships and heroic loves, and the ideals he has pursued down the ages. He sketches an expanding universe, which nevertheless must be always reduced to matter, and whatever happens must be unified under the sign of matter and made intelligible by it. To many this may seem to put an impossible strain not only on the use of the word matter, but on any single and homogeneous sense of it. How, for instance, can a thing be itself and at the same time be the knowledge of itself; and be able to make the identification? If I say that "I am I," I am not only looking at myself but saying that the two are identical, and this on any system of brain states or neurotic circulation or doctrine of relations cannot make sense. Again matter is intelligible as a predictable series of events, which is necessarily determined. Nevertheless we cannot predict with certainty the conduct of individuals or reconcile liberty with necessity without robbing one of the two of its proper meaning. Lastly as matter is the end of all the highest aspirations of man his final happiness must be determined by his economic status. Now in times when people are deprived of their just claims and not given a full opportunity for living a full human life, the sympathy with the grievances and the promise of the removal of these grievances are bound to make a great appeal. Both the oppressed and those of generous mind are stirred at the promise of a new and better society in which these wrongs will be righted. At the same time there is always the danger that reformers may make an appeal to motives of hate, greed, and envy, and the literature of communism is unfortunately full of appeals to such motives. Moreover the appeal usually confines itself to the negative, that is, to the removal of the oppressive social conditions, and it is taken for granted that once this happens all will be well: economic equality and collectivity will bring automatically serene happiness. This is an example of the fallacy that when the tooth stops paining, when I am free of this dull and irksome job, I shall have no cares. There is very little in Communist literature about the positive virtues which will make up the classless society, of courtesy, magnanimity, forbearance, mutual affection, and nothing whatsoever about the interior virtues which the Christian thinks so essential for integrity and highmindedness as well as for mutual relations.

The pattern of life envisaged by communism seems to leave out so much, and even what it contains does not do justice to the parts. The unity of the end and ideal crushes the parts together so that their separate beauty and function are lost. The member of the state cannot for any reason resist its orders or follow his conscience; the novelist, the poet, the philosopher must all subordinate their work to the Communist cause. The Soviet composer, Mura Deli, tried recently to prove that "creative freedom" does exist in the Soviet Union and explained that the "sharp criticism" issued by the Central Committee of the Communist Party against his formalist opera *The Great Friendship* saved him from a "precipice." He had forgotten the rule published on 15 May, 1948, that "only that artist is free in his creations who is versed in the laws of the historical development of society and who with all his heart is devoted to his people, to the Communist Party and to Socialist society."

The literary Rumanian Life published "A Small Handbook for the Creators of Literature." In it the "positive" man must show "force and optimism," to appear "without a tie or pressed trousers." He must be "a virgin up to the time of marriage." The "negative" villain should look like a fox with a long face and be fat. In the last act, if he is a "class enemy" he will "disintegrate in conformity with the laws of history." If he is well off he has to be named Glutton to suggest his rapacity. On the other hand, the Party Secretary in Armenia has recently stated that "the people demand that writers create types which can serve as an example and they have criticized several poets for having depicted under the guise of lyrical love, emotions of decadent, individual-worshiping, puny moods devoid of social significance."

The emphasis on efficiency, the collectivization of the peasants and the planning for heavy industries leave no room for the *Georgics* of a Virgil or the *Canticle to the Sun* of a Francis of Assisi. If it be answered that state supervision is only a phase, and that in the society to come all the free activities of man will be restored, the objection still holds, because this society is laid out on economic lines and the preservation of the economic condition will preclude the revival of the old interests and do nothing to enliven them. Only an end which does not compete with the manifold interests of man can at the same time unite them and leave them free. God is not one object among other objects. So far from that all human values borrow their virtue from his infinite perfection; but just because God is infinitely perfect our human and finite values have room to breathe and to grow. The love of God does not take us away from what is human; it is rather the salt which gives vigor to our human activities. We are prevented, indeed, from falling down and adoring any image, from handing ourselves over body and soul to any führer or dictator or institution. All the multitudinous aims of man are gathered up in an almost Babylonian grandeur of pattern, and the unity is unspoilt by any confusion of one with another or with the dominance of one over the rest. To change the image, we may say that a closed universe gives place to an open one. There is a vast amount to attend to in the affairs of everyday life, in business and in social and political services and at home.

But besides these there are the heights to which the soul of man is drawn, the intimations of something more than temporal and finite, the analogies in knowledge, the inspiration of the muses in art, the unrealized expectation of union in love. The Christian religion gives all these gropings a habitation and a name; it reveals the secret which makes this life intelligible and makes man's passage through time and in history significant and valuable. This secret revealed is to be found in the God of the New Testament, who is not a philosophic absolute or a dark fate or a far-off principle of goodness. He is a living God, creator and sustainer of all nature and life, who so creates that human beings, a reflection of his goodness, are directed to an everlasting end of immortal happiness, which by our graced freedom we can all attain. What he is like is made indelibly clear in the advent of Christ, who is God, and who takes on our human nature. If God is really man, then nothing human can be small or worthless, and we are made certain that all the attempts in history to form a just and happy society are part of the plan of God. The love and worship of him are the gold thread in life, and this gives an incomparable happiness and lifts man up to heights of which he could not conceive left to his own devices; but that very love spills over on to all that is human and makes it also to shine out with an undying beauty. To take one example, which will mark the difference between a materialistic and the Christian philosophy of man, marriage. If man were an animal he would behave in mating like the animal; but in fact he has always sought for something higher, even in primitive times. Love is felt to contain in itself the possibility of perfect union of one flesh and one spirit, and the lines of Troilus in Shakespeare's play express the belief of all true lovers, that a plighted troth will last,

When time is old and hath forgot itself,
When waterdrops have worn the stones of Troy,
And blind oblivion swallowed cities up.

This denial of any dialectic of change, this declaration

of the unchanging constancy of human love at its best does not belong to the Marxist world, where all is change and ideals float on the crest of the dialectic waves. Shakespeare goes on to write of "the winnowed purity of love" and of the "mind that doth renew swifter than blood decays." This is the region of the spirit, which lifts the animal in man up to a higher level, and this humanity in turn is kept vivid and raised even higher by the grace of union with God. The lines of the pre-Christian psalmist are taken up again: "Unless the Lord build the house, they labor in vain that build it," and applied to human society. In the material city honest administration becomes corrupt, authority despotic, organizations bureaucratic, the people a herd and human relations inhuman. A city is built, but "they had brick for stone and slime had they for mortar."

What Christianity and communism have to offer are then as different as heaven from earth, and it would appear that they must meet in a head-on collision; and yet they are both concerned with the welfare of man and can look as if they were brothers. The reason for this likeness may lie in the subconscious ideals which inspire the finest Communist supporters. They do have a belief in man, even though their wished-for resuscitation of him means his death. They believe that man has a vision, and, as Whittaker Chambers says, they summon "mankind to turn its vision into practical reality. On the plane of action, it (communism) summons men to struggle against the inertia of the past which, embodied in social, political, and economic forms, communism claims is blocking the will of mankind to make its next great forward stride." The choice, the same writer thinks, is between God and man, and the Communist has chosen man, and taken the logical step "which three hundred years of rationalism hesitated to take, and said what millions of modern minds think, but do not dare or care to say: If man's mind is the decisive force in the world, what need is there for God? Henceforth man's mind is man's fate." Whatever exaggeration there be in this it does pose the alternatives in a way which makes the antagonism obvious. The two cannot live in the same world.

The Communist recognizes this, and as a consequence he makes it his first object to destroy religion wherever he encounters it. The persecution of religion is not an accident, but a deliberate policy. God is on the side of Christianity, and time seems to favor communism. It is ruthless, no holds are barred, and it employs all the latest methods of intimidation, brainwashing and indoctrination. By placarding religion as evil and its ministers as monsters and by conditioning the mind of the new generation from childhood onward, it is confident that it can create a new kind of mind, which will be immune from the infection of religion. Its successes, moreover, have been made more easy by the inertia and confusion within the ranks of democracy and Christendom. The majority of those who live in the civilization formed by Christianity are no longer aware of its faith. They are divided amongst themselves on the main issues, and many are unwilling to admit the irreligious and materialistic nature of Communist régimes. Christians themselves are, as we have seen, divided in their attitude to Russia and

China, as well as in disagreement amongst themselves. The teaching of religion is often perfunctory, and even more often garbled and uninspiring; a kind of Sunday school lesson which goes in one ear and out of the other. Parents and teachers, who are weak in theory and deficient in practice, drag in religion when the behavior of the young alarms them. Its sole use is to oil the machinery of the state. When religion is taught without conviction and so drably, there can be no rallying of the ranks of Christianity against propagandists who speak "insistently to the human mind at the point where man's hope and man's energy fuse to fierceness." What is old and has lost its novelty is always at a disadvantage even when the new is flimsy and false. The history of thought just as much as the history of dress and art shows how easily diverted and tangential the mind of man is. Christianity has become the familiar of the West, and familiarity has bred, if not contempt, indifference. One hope is that this very indifference has been accompanied with so much ignorance, that the truths of the Christian faith can be so stated as to startle and inspire; and there is also the unique feature of the Christian faith that its riches are such as never to be exhausted.

The plain fact, however, is that these riches are little known. The West does not meet the Communist propaganda against Christianity with an indignant denial. Too many are ill-informed on Christianity or indifferent and so they fall back on "the spirit of democracy" or "the liberty of the people" or other such as rallying cries. They do not realize that what they love and treasure draws its meaning from the Christian philosophy. When they think of religion they remember probably the pale imitation of Christianity taught to them when they were children or the emotional exhortations of preachers who in their person did not command respect. Much, too, that passes for Christianity hardly deserves the name. With such confusion over the very meaning of the Christian faith, and so many divisions and subdivisions, the democratic countries are sorely handicapped, and they have so far fallen back on the uninspiring ideas of a league of nations or a superstate. Nothing will really serve in place of an authentic faith, which gives a meaning and high purpose to life, that is, to every single human life. This Christianity claims to do, but as it is obviously impossible in a short compass to give an adequate account of these claims, I shall confine myself to one point and its corollary. A religious and philosophical explanation should be able to face any human situation, that is, it should be applicable to any human experience. Marxist communism focuses all on a future society, free from all material cares. Christianity is pledged to aiding all moral schemes for the betterment of material conditions, but it is not at all so sure universal material prosperity will bring happiness as a necessary result. Medical science has still a long way to go before it can remove disease and physical suffering, and the curve of psychical troubles does not follow that of the rise and fall of economics. And this is all in the future! Christianity does not pass by the sick, the wounded, the aged, and those broken-hearted by the loss of relatives or friends. The whole world is its stage and there is no experience to which it must shut its eyes. Like the man who on seeing a giraffe said "I do not believe there is such a beast" many philosophies have to deny whole areas of human experience because they can give no meaning to them. Christianity leaves nothing out and has in its calendar of saints men and women of all degrees, the lame and the halt as well as statesmen and solitaries, artists and thieves, bourgeois and proletariat. Alone it gives sense to history or rather to the individuals who come and go to make history. History is the affair of man, or so it seems, and how to make the best of it is the question to which many dusty answers have been given. Even the Communist one, with all its professed optimism, comes to us throught the dust of the ages. But, for it is time to conclude with the supreme answer of Christian faith—Christ, the Son of God, lived in history and has no dust where he has trod. All disputes about the Christian religion in its relation to history and in its conflict with communism turn ultimately on the answer to the question whether Christ was what he said he was. If it be true that he was and is both God and Man, then it is not a fantasy to believe that what is human, so long as it is attached in some way to the historical humanity of Christ, is also caught up above time into eternity. Eternity of everlasting life is not a negative notion as of endless continuation. It is positive and means, at least, that it is ever present, and turning every passing moment into something consummate. No matter, therefore, when a human being lives and no matter in what year or condition, he can be "made perfect" and have, as the Fourth Gospel says, everlasting life. To be sure, each individual in his freedom can say yes or no to the grace of the new life, and the importance of this choice cannot be exaggerated. But he is free from the sense of futility, or fate, or of living in an indifferent or hostile universe. The Gospel speaks of judgment, but that judgment is one of love. The God-man is Agapé itself and his whole purpose is to be the light which shines on *every* man and the love which redeems and reconciles the world to God. That being so, instead of the lives of men and women in successive generations being considered as a kind of scaffolding for a future building, each is a mansion in itself. In my Father's palace there are many mansions; and instead of a series of links in a chain, each individual is a pearl of great price in the necklace of history. In the Christian conception of man and his history "out come all his roughness, all his dullness, all his incapability; shame upon shame, failure upon failure, pause after pause; but out comes the whole majesty of man also; and we know the height of it only when we see the clouds settling upon him. And, whether the clouds be bright or dark, there will be transfiguration behind and within them" (Ruskin's *Stones of Venice*).

As the divine, therefore, is ever in the present stamping the coinage of Caesar or Charlemagne or Lincoln into the inscription of Christ, we have to beware of the tendency to put off all in history to a future end. Let it be granted that there is a growth in civilization and a city to be built, but this can come about only by concentration on the individual's worth, and perhaps in and through the Christian message of the promise of divine love to all alike. The supernatural vocation of the individual is what salvages social and civil life. To

both the tramp and the economic philosopher are the
words of Christ addressed:

> *Thy place is built above the starres clear;*
> *None other palace built in such stately wise.*
> *Come on my friend, my brother most entire,*
> *For thee I offered up my blood in sacrifice.*

Bibliographical Note

The writings on communism are too vast for me to attempt a bibliography. Instead I give a list of recent
books, which are not too technical nor too large, and
bear on the subject of communism and Christianity.

Christian Faith and Communist Faith, edited by
Professor D. M. MacKinnon, and including essays by
H. A. Hodges, Professor of Philosophy in the Univer-
sity of Reading; Denys L. Munby, Lecturer in Eco-
nomics in the University of Aberdeen; M. J. Foster
and I. M. Crombie. *Communism and Christ,* by Dr.
Charles W. Lowry. *Communism and Man,* by F. J.
Sheed. *Creative Society,* by J. Macmurray. *The Chris-*

tian Significance of Karl Marx, by Alexander Miller. *Marxism, An Interpretation,* by Alasdair C. MacIntyre. *Karl Marx,* by I. Berlin. *What Is Marxism?* by Emile Burns. *Social Thinking,* by Hyman Levy. *Catholic Social Principles,* by Lewis Watt. *What Is Communism?* by J. Plamenatz. *I Believed: Answer to Communism,* by Douglas Hyde.